D0623745

From Raindrops to Roses

A Collection of Oregon Style Celebrations

**JUNIOR LEAGUE OF
PORTLAND, OR**
Women building better communities

Photos provided courtesy of:

Jon Conant-*10*

Ruth Gaunt-*35, 42, 50, 56, 79, 94, 108, 113*

Margaret Heald-*14, 16, 24, 37, 39, 52, 58, 67, 70, 73, 77, 86, 114, 124*

GBD Architects-*83*

Kim Nguyen-Cover, *4, 6, 32, 92, 104, 119, 121*
www.photosbykim.com

Metschan Media-*30*

Duane Morris Photography-*88*

www.pioneercourthousesquare.org

The Oregon Historical Society-*46*

The Oregon Shakespeare Festival-*82*

The Oregon Zoo-*105*

From Raindrops to Roses
A Collection of Oregon Style Celebrations

Published and written by the Junior League of Portland, Oregon Inc.

Copyright © 2005 by the Junior League of Portland, Oregon, Inc.
842 SW 1st Avenue
Portland, Oregon 97204
503-203-2372
info@juniorleagueofportland.net | www.juniorleagueofportland.org

This cookbook is a collection of favorite recipes, which are not necessarily original recipes.

All rights reserved. No part of this publication may be reproduced in any form or by any means, electronic or mechanical, including photocopy and information storage and retrieval systems, without permission in writing, from the publisher.

The proceeds generated from the sale of From Raindrops to Roses - A Collection of Oregon Style Celebrations and From Portland's Palate - A Collection of Recipes from the City of Roses will support the purpose and programs of the Junior League of Portland, Oregon, Incorporated, a 501 (C) (3), nonprofit organization.

Library of Congress Control Number: 2005929318
ISBN: 0-9632525-2-6

Designed by IDL Merchandising Solutions
319 SW Washington, Suite 500
Portland, Oregon 97204-2622
503-224-8160

Manufactured by CDS Publications
A Consolidated Graphics Company
2661 South Pacific Highway
Medford, Oregon 97501
541-773-7575

Editor-in-Chief: Kaycee Wiita
Project Editors: Barbra Jorgensen, Erica Hetfeld, Dana Plautz and Angie Regali
Design Editors: Teresa Forni and Gretchen Anderson Pilip
Recipe Editors: JoAnna Flynn, Kristin Hedman, Mandy Magaddino, and Kristin Riddle
Book Design: Ruth Gaunt, Margaret Heald, and Diana Schreiber
Cover Design, Food and Set Stylists: Teresa Forni and Pamela Kearney

Manufactured in the United States of America
Second Printing: 2006

Major Contributors:

Special thanks to the following businesses and people who donated their time and talent to From Raindrops to Roses - A Collection of Oregon Style Celebrations:

Dr. and Mrs. Robert Pamplin Jr.

Cover - Teresa and Rodney Forni for graciously giving us access to their beautiful home for photos in this cookbook.

Design and Layout - Ruth Gaunt-Margaret Heald-Diana Schreiber and IDL Merchandising Solutions

Cookbook Research Committee 2003-2004

Anne Bell-Kathy Brandeberry-Jennifer Butts-Andrea Costello
Holly Eddins-Cathie Ericson-Teresa Forni-Hallie Janssen-Diane Keaton
Deidre Krys-Rusoff-Lisa Perrin-Deanna Phillips-Gretchen Pilip-Tori Pontrelli
Angie Regali-Tristan Ritter-Denise Weissman-Kaycee Wiita-Christine Zieverink

Cookbook Development Committee 2004-2005

Rhonda Beck-Anne Bell-Channing Bosler-Kathy Brandeberry-Ophelia Chiu
Dina Cole-Michelle Doherty-JoAnna Flynn-Teresa Forni-Frances Rhee Hamrick
Kristin Hedman-Erica Hetfeld-Nancy Janney-Barbra Jorgensen-Mandy Magaddino
Christin Peterson-Gretchen Pilip-Debbie Richman-Kristin Riddle-Anne Ryan
Donna Smalldon-Kaycee Wiita-Christine Zieverink

Cookbook Marketing Committee 2005-2006

Channing Bosler-Kristen Buonpane-Amy Checkman-Dina Sue Cole
Andrea Costello-Michelle Doherty-JoAnna Flynn-Cari Goodwin-Wendy Herrero
Erica Hetfeld-Heather Leek-Pamela Lindberg-Jennifer Lynch-Mandy Magaddino
Tina Pisenti-Kristin Riddle-Amber Stinson-Kaycee Wiita-Christine Zieverink

Kathy Brandeberry	Kaycee Wiita	Erica Hetfeld
Cookbook Chair 2003-2004	*Cookbook Chair 2004-2005*	*Cookbook Chair 2005-2006*
Kaycee Wiita	Barbra Jorgensen	Channing Bosler
President 2003-2004	*President 2004-2005*	*President 2005-2006*

From Raindrops to Roses
A Collection of Oregon Style Celebrations

Creators Of:

From Portland's Palate - A Collection of Recipes from the City of Roses
Winner of the prestigious 1993 Tabasco Community Cookbook Award

To purchase copies of **From Raindrops to Roses - A Collection of Oregon Style Celebrations**, visit us online at www.juniorleagueofportland.org, complete the order form in the back of the book, or call the Junior League of Portland, Oregon at 503-203-2372

Mission:

The Junior League of Portland, Oregon, Inc. is an organization of women committed to promoting voluntarism, developing the potential of women and improving communities through trained volunteers. Its purpose is exclusively educational and charitable. The Junior League of Portland reaches out to all women who demonstrate an interest in and commitment to voluntarism.

A History of Outreach and Giving

Women Building Better Communities

In 1910, a transplanted New Yorker and member of the City of New York Junior League, Gretchen Hoyt Corbett, realized her new city had many of the same immigration, industrialization and urbanization issues she recognized from home. Corbett mobilized first her sewing circle, and then a larger group, to tackle child labor, tuberculosis and safe food supply issues for impoverished women and children in Portland. This group became the Junior League of Portland and is the fourth oldest Junior League in the world.

During the first and second World Wars, the League dispatched volunteers all over Portland to serve in hospital or fundraising settings. In WWII, the League developed Portland's first central volunteer defense bureau, that soon became the city's official female volunteer clearinghouse.

Through the 50s and 60s the League concentrated on educational and cultural projects, getting involved with local radio, arts and women's leadership projects in concert with other Portland non-profits. The League took on diversity, historic preservation and supported programs for the developmentally disabled in the 70s and literacy and child advocacy works in the following decade. In the 1990s, the League officially targeted basic needs for women and children.

Current Junior League of Portland community projects include:

Between The Lines - A ground breaking program that the JLP facilitates at a Portland-area prison to give children of incarcerated mothers books and a tape of their mother reading the book to them. The goal of this program is to help stop the cycle of children of incarcerated parents ending up behind bars themselves. This unique program connects incarcerated women with their children.

Done In a Day - Assisting other nonprofits with fundraising and community events. **LifeSkills** - Empowering the daily lives of homeless women and children - women escaping addiction and domestic violence at local shelters. **Art Works** - Provides a creative outlet for young victims of child abuse and "at-risk" children, helping facilitate a healthy development process through art activities with volunteer mentors. **Training our Members to be Nonprofit Leaders** - Training women to become leaders in nonprofit leadership and management.

Past projects brought to Portland by the Junior League include: The Boys' & Girls' Aid Society, the Fruit & Flower Mission, Race For The Cure, Kids On The Block, YWCA Transitional School For Homeless Children, CASA, The Ronald McDonald House, West Women's Shelter, Parry Center For Children, Habitat For Humanity, Christie School and The Dougy Center. These are just a few of the many organizations in the community that now stand on their own because of the Junior League.

The Junior League of Portland's membership consists of women from all backgrounds who have joined our organization to learn about effective voluntarism and to make an impact on the community. League members are trained in numerous areas including volunteering in the community, leadership, fundraising, project development and diversity. Active and sustaining members are found on numerous nonprofit boards in the Portland metropolitan area where their Junior League leadership training is a valuable asset.

The Junior League of Portland is a member of the Association of Junior Leagues International with over 170,000 members in 294 Leagues in the United States, Canada, Great Britain and Mexico.

TABLE OF CONTENTS

The Menus

Lover's Lane
Curried Carrot and Parsnip Soup
Couch Street Scallops with Saffron Sauce
Reedsport Wild Rice
Heavenly Ginger Crème Brulee

Rose Parade Rendezvous
Dragon Boat Chile Pepper Shrimp
Hells Canyon Fish Tacos with Guacamole and Corn Salsa
Double Chocolate Cherry Drops

Sunriver Soiree
Rose Garden Iced Wine
Baked Brie Quesadillas with Mango and Avocado Salsa
Peach and Tomato Salad with Cilantro Lime Vinaigrette
Columbia River Grilled Salmon with Blueberry Sauce
Blackberry Ice Cream Pie

Golden Sunset Supper
Pacific Golden Chanterelle and Goat Cheese Crostini
Sauvie Island Tomato Soup with Basil Cream
Apple Stuffed Pork Loin with Raspberry Sauce
Chilled Apricot Torte

Lighting Pioneer Square
Pear and Hazelnut Baked Brie
Lewis and Clark Herb Roasted Lamb with Pinot Noir Sauce
Dijon and Brown Sugar Glazed Carrots
Herbed Potato Soufflé
Pear Tart

First Thursday Dinner in the Pearl
Sun-Dried Tomato Pesto with Toast Points
Hazelnut and Gorgonzola Salad
Crab and Chanterelle Chowder
Duniway Chocolate Cake

Crystal Nights

Lover's Lane

Curried Carrot and Parsnip Soup

Couch Street Scallops *with Saffron Sauce*

Reedsport Wild Rice

Heavenly Ginger Crème Brulee

In the winter, west traveling air swirling through the Cascade Mountains via the Columbia River Gorge brings cold air from the interior of the state westward to Portland. At the same time, incoming east traveling rain that comes from the west hits the cold air from central Oregon resulting in freezing rain and dazzling crystal nights!

While the roads can be treacherous the sight of icicles hanging from trees, and eaves around the beautifully lit city are stunning! Portlanders gather together with friends and family to enjoy these spectacular shows of nature over an elegant but casual meal paired with a rich pinot noir from Oregon's famous wine region in the Willamette Valley. While the ice melts in the valleys, Oregon's mountains are filled with snow that offers a variety of outdoor recreation. Oregonians, who are known for their enjoyment of the outdoors, head for the mountains or the sea to enjoy everything from downhill skiing, to storm watching on the coast!

Newport Shrimp with Roasted Pepper and Horseradish Dip

Prep time: 30 minutes
Cook time: 15 minutes

Dip:

4   large red bell peppers (about 2 pounds)
3   tablespoons low-fat sour cream
3   tablespoons prepared horseradish
1   tablespoon olive oil
2   teaspoons fresh lemon juice
½   teaspoon salt
¼   teaspoon black pepper
2   garlic cloves, chopped

1. Cut bell peppers in half lengthwise; discard seeds and membranes.
2. Place pepper halves, skin side up, on a foil-lined baking sheet; flatten with hand.
3. Broil 15 minutes or until blackened.
4. Place in a zip-top plastic bag and seal. Let stand 15 minutes. Peel peppers.
5. Place bell peppers, sour cream, horseradish, olive oil, lemon juice, salt, pepper and garlic in a food processor and process until smooth.
6. Place bell pepper mixture in a small bowl. Cover and chill.
7. Serve with cooked and peeled shrimp.

Shrimp:

2   pounds large, cooked and peeled shrimp

Yield: 8 servings

Hawthorne Avenue
Black Bean Soup

Prep time: 15 minutes
Cook time: 40 minutes

Soup:

1   tablespoon olive oil
1   medium onion, chopped
1   cup green bell pepper, chopped
½   cup red bell pepper, chopped
1   cup carrots, sliced
4   cups chicken broth
1   21 ounce jar of mild or medium salsa
1   15 ounce can of corn, drained
2   15 ounce cans of black beans, rinsed and drained
1   15 ounce can of diced tomatoes
¼   cup cilantro, chopped
     sour cream to taste

1. In a large saucepan, sauté the onion in olive oil over medium heat for 5 to 7 minutes.
2. Add green bell pepper, red bell pepper and carrots; sauté 5 minutes or until soft.
3. Add chicken broth, salsa, corn, beans and tomatoes. Slowly bring to a boil and then reduce heat to low.
4. Cover and simmer soup for 15 to 20 minutes, stirring frequently.
5. Add cilantro, reserving some for garnish.
6. Ladle soup into bowls. Serve with sour cream and additional cilantro.

Yield: 6 servings

PORTLAND'S BED AND BREAKFAST INNS

For those wanting a night off from the ordinary or are looking to visit Portland, but want a home-like atmosphere, Portland offers numerous bed and breakfasts right in town.

Portland's White House

This former residence of a lumber baron appears strikingly like a scaled-down version of the White House in Washington D.C. The Irvington neighborhood's White House features eight guest rooms and an extensive collection of 19th century oil paintings and porcelain.

CURRIED CARROT AND PARSNIP SOUP

Prep time: 15 minutes
Cook time: 1 hour

SOUP:

10	carrots cut into ½ inch pieces
3	parsnips cut into ½ inch pieces
2	medium onions cut into ½ inch pieces
3	quarts chicken broth
5	teaspoons curry powder
1	14 ounce jar orange marmalade
2	cups heavy whipping cream or half and half
	curry powder to taste

1. Place the carrots, parsnips, onions, broth and curry powder in a 5-quart pot and bring to a boil.
2. Reduce heat to medium high and cook until vegetables are soft.
3. Remove from heat and cool for 15 minutes.
4. Place the mixture in a food processor. Process until texture is smooth but somewhat coarse. This may be done in batches.
4. Return mixture to pot. Reheat the soup.
5. Add the marmalade and whipping cream, stirring to combine. Add curry to taste. Serve piping hot.

Yield: 6 servings

MIXED GREENS WITH BRANDIED BRIE AND PEAR CROSTINI

Prep time: 60 minutes
Broil: 4-8 minutes

BRIE:

4	ounces Brie cheese
1	tablespoon unsalted butter
2	tablespoons brandy
¼	cup pecans, chopped

1. Place Brie cheese and butter in a medium size bowl and let stand for 30 minutes.
2. Combine Brie cheese and butter.
3. Stir in brandy and chopped pecans and set aside.

CROSTINI:

16 ¼ inch thick baguette slices

1. Place bread slices on a baking sheet and broil until golden brown, turning once to brown other side.

DRESSING:

1	teaspoon salt	1	clove garlic, minced
½	teaspoon ground black pepper	5	tablespoons raspberry vinegar
¼	teaspoon sugar	½	cup vegetable oil
½	teaspoon dry mustard	2	tablespoons extra-virgin olive oil
	juice of ½ lemon		

1. Mix salt, pepper, sugar, mustard, lemon, garlic and vinegar together.
2. Slowly add vegetable oil and olive oil until blended. Set aside.

ASSEMBLING:

1 medium size pear, cored and thinly sliced
4 cups mixed greens, washed and dried

1. Top each toasted bread slice with a pear slice.
2. Top each pear slice with 1 tablespoon of Brie cheese mixture.
3. Broil until cheese is melted and bubbly.
4. Place salad greens in bowl and toss with desired amount of dressing.
5. Divide salad among 4-6 salad plates and place a brandied Brie and pear crostini in the center and serve immediately.

Yield: 4-6 servings

The Lion and the Rose Victorian Bed and Breakfast

This B&B is a 1906 Queen Anne Victorian mansion situated close to chic shops and restaurants in Northeast Portland. The Lion and the Rose has been added to the National Register of Historic Places and has six guest rooms all with in-suite bathrooms.

The MacMaster House

This Southwest Portland B&B is located within walking distance to the upscale shopping district on Northwest 23rd Avenue and a short ride into downtown. The MacMaster House is also close to Portland's famous Rose Garden and peaceful Washington Park. Most rooms have romantic fireplaces.

TIMBERLINE LODGE

Anyone who noticed the ski lodge in the film "The Shining" has experienced a little taste of Timberline Lodge. The lodge is a warm, rustic slice of history that has sat on the slopes of Mt. Hood just east of Portland since the Federal Works Progress Administration finished construction in 1937. Craftsmen built the entire lodge by hand, which is part of the reason why Timberline was declared a National Historic Landmark in 1978.

Nowadays, snow lovers from all over the world come to Timberline to ski, snowboard or just have a hot drink and take in the alpine views. Visitors are welcome any time of year because Timberline boasts one of the longest ski seasons in the nation.

Although the mountain is the main attraction, the lodge itself is a beautiful structure to visit. Art is present in every detail, from the mosaic floor in the foyer, to subtle carvings in the beams and hand-made wrought iron door handles. A documentary detailing the building of the lodge is on continuous loop in the main lobby. Timberline features a formal dining room, lodging, gift shops and year-round skiing all within two hours of Portland.

REEDSPORT WILD RICE

Prep time: 20 minutes
Cook time: 45 minutes
Oven: 350 degrees

RICE:

3   tablespoons butter
1   small yellow onion, chopped
4   ounces mushrooms, sliced
¼   cup uncooked wild rice
1   medium rib celery, chopped (½ cup)
½   teaspoon salt
¼   teaspoon fresh sage, chopped
¼   teaspoon fresh basil, chopped
2½   cups chicken broth
¾   cup uncooked long grain rice
1   cup sour cream
1   tablespoon fresh parsley, chopped

1. Preheat oven to 350 degrees.
2. Melt butter in a medium sized skillet over medium low heat.
3. Sauté onions and mushrooms until onion is tender and mushrooms are cooked.
4. Add wild rice, celery, salt, sage and basil.
5. Pour wild rice mixture into an un-greased 1½ quart oven-safe casserole.
6. Heat broth to boiling; pour over wild rice mixture.
7. Stir in long grain rice. Cover and bake for 40 to 45 minutes, or until liquid is absorbed and rice is tender.
8. Stir in sour cream, sprinkle with parsley and serve immediately.

Yield: 6 servings

Oven-Roasted Winter Root Vegetables

Prep time: 20 minutes
Cook time: 45 minutes
Oven: 450 degrees

Vegetables:

3   cups potatoes (fingerling, new or purple), washed and cut into 1 inch cubes
3   cups butternut squash, peeled and cut into 1 inch cubes
12   cloves garlic, peeled and diced
8   shallots, peeled and halved lengthwise
1   tablespoon fresh sage, chopped
¼   cup maple syrup
¼   cup olive oil
       kosher salt and fresh ground pepper to taste

1. Preheat oven to 450 degrees.
2. Combine potatoes, squash, garlic, shallots, sage, syrup and olive oil in a large mixing bowl adding enough oil and syrup to evenly coat the vegetables. Season generously with salt and pepper.
3. Place in a large roasting pan or casserole in one, even layer.
4. Roast, stirring every 10 minutes, until vegetables are tender and garlic and shallots are tender, 30 to 45 minutes.

Yield: 6 servings

Cauliflower with Prosciutto and Swiss Cheese

Prep time: 15 minutes
Cook time: 45 minutes
Oven: 350 degrees

6   tablespoons unsalted butter
6   cloves garlic, peeled and minced
4   ounces thinly sliced prosciutto, cut into thin strips
1   large head of cauliflower, cut lengthwise into ¼ inch slices
2   tablespoons unbleached all-purpose flour
1½   cups heavy cream or whipping cream
1   pinch ground red pepper
       salt and freshly ground pepper
1½   cups Swiss cheese, grated

1.   Preheat oven to 350 degrees.
2.   Melt the butter in a large skillet over medium heat. Add garlic and sauté for 2 minutes. Stir in prosciutto and sauté 2 minutes.
3.   Add the cauliflower and cook until just tender, 3 to 5 minutes.
4.   Stir in flour and cream and blend well. Season with red pepper, salt and ground black pepper.
5.   Bring to a boil and remove from heat.
6.   Pour cauliflower into a shallow casserole.
7.   Tent with foil and bake for 30 minutes.
8.   Uncover, top with cheese and bake until the cheese is lightly browned and bubbling. Serve immediately.

Yield: 6 servings

Couch Street Scallops with Saffron Sauce

Prep time: 5 minutes
Cook time: 25 minutes

Scallops:

2   tablespoons butter
20   large sea scallops

1. Melt butter in a large pan.
2. Add scallops and cook on medium heat for 2 to 3 minutes. Transfer scallops to a warm plate.

Wine Sauce:

1½   cups dry white wine
      pinch of saffron threads
1   cup whipping cream
1   teaspoon vanilla extract
2   tablespoons lemon juice
      salt and pepper to taste

1. Add wine and saffron to pan and boil until reduced by half.
2. Add cream, vanilla and lemon juice. Boil until reduced to a smooth consistency, about 10 minutes and season with salt and pepper.
3. Add scallops to warm mixture.
4. Transfer to a warm plate and serve immediately.

Yield: 6 servings

THE NEWPORT SEAFOOD AND WINE FESTIVAL

This central coast town doubles in size for a weekend each February during the Newport Seafood and Wine Festival. This party started in 1978 and features over 120 wine vendors, about half of which feature Oregon wines. The seafood is also plentiful, as festival goers can pick through local specialties like prawn cocktails, salmon quesadillas and tuna kabobs.

The weekend's main event is the commercial wine competition, during which oenologists, wine writers, sommeliers and restaurateurs judge wines in a variety of categories, and from those categories comes a Best in Show.

MT. BACHELOR SAUSAGE, CLAMS AND POTATOES

Prep time: 30 minutes
Cook time: 20 minutes

SAUSAGE AND CLAMS:

½	pound red potatoes, washed and diced
1	tablespoon olive oil
½	pound ground Italian sausage, mild or spicy
8	cloves of garlic, coarsely chopped
1	cup white wine
1	cup chicken or fish stock
1	pound whole clams, well-scrubbed
¼	cup flat leaf parsley, chopped
	sea salt and fresh ground pepper to taste
	French bread, sliced, rubbed with garlic and toasted for serving

1. Boil potatoes until tender. Remove from heat and drain.
2. In a large stockpot, brown sausage.
3. Add garlic and sauté about 30 seconds.
4. Add potatoes, wine and stock and bring to a boil.
5. Add clams, cover and simmer until the shells have opened, about 5 minutes. Remove the clams and discard the shells.
6. Stir in parsley, season with salt and pepper. Serve in large bowls over the bread.

Yield: 4 servings

Hazelnut Crusted Sautéed Chicken

Prep time: 20 minutes
Cook time: 20 minutes
Oven: 350 degrees

Hazelnut Chicken:

¾   cup hazelnuts
1½   cup fresh, unseasoned bread crumbs
2   eggs, lightly beaten
4   boneless skinless chicken breast halves (about 1½ pounds)
½   cup all-purpose flour
½   teaspoon sea salt
½   teaspoon freshly ground white pepper
¼   cup butter, clarified
¼   cup grape seed oil (or vegetable, or canola)

1. Preheat oven to 350 degrees.
2. Heat hazelnuts in a dry skillet over medium heat, stirring frequently to prevent burning, until they just begin to release their fragrance, about 4 minutes. Cool, and chop finely.
3. In a shallow casserole, combine hazelnuts and bread crumbs.
4. Lightly beat eggs in a separate dish.
5. Place chicken between two sheets of waxed paper and pound to ½ inch thickness.
6. In a bowl, combine flour, salt and pepper. Dredge chicken breasts and shake off excess flour.
7. Dip chicken in the egg mixture, and then the hazelnut and bread crumb mixture.
8. In a large skillet, heat butter and oil over medium high heat. Sauté chicken 3 to 4 minutes on each side until browned. Remove to an oven-safe plate lined with paper towels.
9. Bake for 10 to 15 minutes. Remove from oven, allow to rest 5 minutes, and serve.

Yield: 4 servings

Filet Mignon with Balsamic Glaze and Goat Cheese

Prep time: 10 minutes
Cook time: 25 minutes

Balsamic Glaze:

1½   cups balsamic vinegar
3   tablespoons sugar

1. In a small heavy saucepan, bring the balsamic vinegar and sugar to a boil over medium high heat, stirring occasionally, about 18 minutes. Set aside.

Filet Mignon:

2   tablespoons butter
6   5 to 6 ounce filet mignon steaks, each about 1 inch thick
       salt and pepper to taste
2   ounces fresh goat cheese

1. Preheat the broiler.
2. Melt the butter in a large heavy skillet over medium high heat.
3. Sprinkle the steaks with salt and pepper.
4. Sauté the steaks in skillet to desired degree of doneness, about 3 minutes per side for medium rare. Transfer the steaks to a baking sheet.
5. Crumble the cheese over the steaks and broil until the cheese melts, about 1 minute. Sprinkle with salt and pepper.
6. Transfer the steaks to plates, drizzle the balsamic vinegar glaze around the steaks and serve.

Yield: 6 servings

Blueberry French Toast

Prep time: 15 minutes
Cook time: 60 minutes
Marinate: Overnight
Oven: 350 degrees

French Toast:

12   slices French bread, cut into 1 inch cubes
12   ounces cream cheese, cut into ½ inch cubes
1   cup blueberries
12   eggs
2   cups milk
1½ cups maple syrup

1. Grease a 9 x 13 baking dish.
2. Place half the bread cubes in the pan and top with cream cheese and blueberries.
3. Arrange the remaining bread cubes over the top.
4. In a large bowl, lightly beat the eggs. Add milk and maple syrup and stir until combined.
5. Pour egg mixture over bread, cover with foil and refrigerate overnight.
6. Preheat oven to 350 degrees.
7. Bake, covered, for 30 minutes. Remove foil and bake an additional 30 minutes.
8. Serve with blueberry syrup.

Blueberry Syrup:

1   cup sugar
2   tablespoons cornstarch
1   cup water
1   cup blueberries

1. In a small saucepan, combine sugar, cornstarch and water. Bring to a low boil over medium high heat.
2. Cook, stirring constantly, 5 minutes or until thickened.
3. Add blueberries and simmer 10 minutes or until most berries have burst.

Yield: 12 servings

CRAB AND ARTICHOKE FRITTATA

Prep time: 15 minutes
Cook time: 45-60 minutes
Oven: 350 degrees

FRITATTA:

2   tablespoons butter
8   ounces button mushrooms, scrubbed, and sliced
5   eggs, beaten
1   cup sour cream
1   cup small curd cottage cheese, blended in a food processor
½   cup grated Parmesan cheese
¼   cup flour
1   teaspoon onion powder
⅛   teaspoon salt
4   drops Tabasco sauce
1   cup flaked crab
2   cups Monterey Jack cheese
1   14.5 ounce can non-marinated artichoke hearts, drained and quartered

1. Preheat oven to 350 degrees.
2. Sauté mushrooms in butter. Drain on a paper towel.
3. Blend eggs, sour cream, cottage cheese, Parmesan cheese, flour, onion powder, salt and Tabasco in a large bowl. Add sautéed mushrooms, crab, Monterey Jack cheese, and artichoke hearts.
4. Pour into a greased 10-inch quiche pan or pie plate.
5. Bake 45-60 minutes or until a knife inserted into the center of the frittata comes out clean.
6. Remove from oven and let stand 5 minutes before serving.

Yield: 8 servings

Northwest's Best Oatmeal Cookies

Prep time: 15 minutes
Cook time: 15 minutes
Oven: 350 degrees

Cookies:

1½   cups butter, softened
1   cup granulated sugar
1½   cups light brown sugar, firmly packed
3   eggs
1   tablespoon vanilla
3   cups all purpose flour
1   tablespoon baking powder
1   teaspoon salt
1   tablespoon ground cinnamon
½   teaspoon ground nutmeg
3   cups quick cooking oatmeal
2   cups walnuts, chopped
1   12 ounce bag semi-sweet chocolate chips
2   cups dried cranberries

1. Preheat oven to 350 degrees.
2. Cream butter and sugars. Beat in eggs and vanilla.
3. Add flour, baking powder, salt, cinnamon, nutmeg and oatmeal, slowly beating until blended. Stir in walnuts, chocolate chips and cranberries.
4. Drop by spoonfuls onto a cookie sheet covered with wax paper. Shape drops into rounds.
5. Bake 12 to 15 minutes or until golden brown.

Yield: 8 dozen cookies

Oregon's Winter Playgrounds

Oregon has 10 lift-served ski areas in every corner of the state, where Oregonians can be found enjoying a multitude of winter activities.

The Northern Cascades

Timberline, Mt. Hood Meadows, Mt. Hood Ski Bowl and Cooper Spur ski areas all sit on or near Mt. Hood and are all around an hour and a half from Portland. Between them, a snow lover can take in snowshoeing, skiing on black diamond or bunny trails, cross-country skiing, inner tubing, seasonal sleigh rides, snowboarding in a "pipe park" and night skiing.

The Central Cascades

Mt. Bachelor, Hoodoo and Willamette Pass are all located near the Bend and Eugene areas. Willamette Pass features Oregon's first six-seat chair lift while Hoodoo sits near Black Butte Ranch, one of Oregon's premier resorts. Mt. Bachelor is the largest ski area in the state and a favorite destination for highly skilled skiers.

Snowblast Brandy Pie

Prep time: 20 minutes
Freeze time: 2 hours

Pie Crust:

20	whole graham crackers, crushed (four squares per cracker)
3	tablespoons brown sugar
⅓	cup butter, soft

1. Combine graham cracker crumbs, brown sugar and butter. Press into a 9 inch pie pan and chill.

Filling:

1	cup heavy cream
½	cup powdered confectioner's sugar, sifted
¼	cup brandy
4	egg yolks
	additional graham cracker crumbs for topping

1. With an electric mixer, beat cream until stiff. Stir in powdered sugar and brandy at low speed.
2. In a small bowl, beat egg yolks until light colored and thick. Fold into cream mixture, then pour filling into chilled crust.
3. Freeze for 30 minutes, top with plain graham cracker crumbs.
4. Freeze until hardened, at least another 1 ½ hours.
5. Slice with a warm knife. Serve frozen.

Yield: 6 to 8 servings

Heavenly Ginger Crème Brulee

Prep time: 1 hour
Cook time: 45 minutes
Chill: Overnight
Oven: 325 degrees

Crème Brulee:

3¼   cups whipping cream
2   tablespoons ginger, peeled and coarsely grated
10   large egg yolks
1¼   cups sugar
        strawberries or star fruit to garnish
        fresh mint

1. Preheat oven to 325 degrees.
2. Combine cream and ginger in a medium saucepan. Bring to a simmer over medium heat. Remove from heat and let stand 25 minutes.
3. Strain cream into a small bowl, pressing on solids in the sieve.
4. Whisk egg yolks and 1 cup sugar in a medium bowl. Gradually whisk in the cream mixture.
5. Divide the custard among 6, ¾ cup ramekins or custard cups.
6. Place ramekins in a large roasting pan. Pour enough warm water into the pan to come halfway up the sides of the ramekins.
7. Bake custards just until set in the center when the pan is gently shaken, about 45 minutes.
8. Remove custards from the water bath. Chill uncovered until cold, about 3 hours.
9. Cover and chill overnight.
10. Preheat broiler, or use a culinary torch.
11. Place custards on a baking sheet. Sprinkle each with ½ teaspoon sugar.
12. Broil or torch until sugar melts and caramelizes, turning the baking sheet for even browning, about 1 minute.
13. Garnish with fruit and mint and serve.

Yield: 6 servings

The Siskiyous

Mt. Ashland is a community-owned operation just south of Ashland on the California border. Four chair lifts serve 23 groomed runs, and at the 7,500 foot summit you can take in Siskiyou mountain views.

Eastern Oregon

Warner Canyon and Anthony Lakes ski areas sit in the frontier areas of Oregon. Anthony Lakes, which is a relatively small area, is located between Baker City and LaGrande and enjoys the driest snowfall in the state. Warner Canyon is tucked into arid Southeastern Oregon and is great for a low-cost family day on the mountain.

Mrs. Stolee's Rum Cake

Prep time: 30 minutes
Cook time: 60 minutes
Oven: 325 degrees

Cake:

1   package yellow or golden butter cake mix
1   3.4 ounce package instant vanilla pudding
½   cup light rum
½   cup vegetable oil
½   cup water
4   eggs

1. Preheat oven to 325 degrees. Grease and flour a bundt pan.
2. Combine cake mix, pudding, rum, oil, water and eggs in a large bowl and beat 2 minutes with an electric mixer.
3. Pour into pan; bake 50 to 60 minutes.

Glaze:

½   cup butter
½   cup granulated sugar
¼   cup rum
¼   cup water

1. Combine butter, sugar, rum and water in a small heavy saucepan.
2. Bring to a boil and cook 2 to 3 minutes.
3. Pour over the hot cake.

Yield: 12 servings

When Raindrops Fall

Rose Parade Rendezvous

Dragon Boat Chile Pepper Shrimp

Hells Canyon Fish Tacos *with Guacamole and Corn Salsa*

Double Chocolate Cherry Drops

Portland area residents know what causes all the commotion in town every year in June. Since 1907, the Portland Rose Festival has brought the community together for parades, events, food and entertainment. We don't call Portland "The City of Roses" for nothing.

The Rose Festival has been named the most highly decorated event or festival in the world by the International Festivals and Events Association.

Families can enjoy the Festival's annual events including; the Grand Floral Parade, The Starlight Parade, the Waterfront Village Carnival, the Festival of Bands, the Rose Festival Queen's Coronation, the Rose Show, the Indy Car Race at the Portland International Raceway, the Golden Rose Ski Classic, fireworks over the waterfront, Dragon Boat Races and the art festival. During the rest of the year, the Festival's "Royal Rosarians" serve as the city's official ambassadors. This group of community leaders is easily recognizable by the all-white suits, shoes and hats they don at every public appearance.

Portlanders always find time during this wonderful coming of spring to gather together with fabulous food and friends to celebrate the cultural bounty that Portland offers.

Dragon Boat Racing

Chinese dragon boat races are a symbol of Chinese culture and spirit. Each year, the Rose Festival hosts the Portland-Kaohsiung Sister City Association Dragon Boat Races. Always exotic and exciting, more than 100 teams compete (including local, national and international teams) with heats of four teams competing every six to eight minutes.

The boats, which are provided through the Portland-Kaohsiung Sister City Association, are long, multicolored boats with frightening dragons' heads, long tails and scaly bodies. The races symbolize man's struggle against nature and his fight against dangerous enemies and have been in existence for more than 2000 years.

The Dragon Boat Races are held on the Willamette River near the Hawthorne Bridge. Spectators watch the races at the south end of Tom McCall Waterfront Park.

Dragon Boat Chile Pepper Shrimp

Prep time: 25 minutes
Cook time: 3-5 minutes
Marinate: 4 hours
Boil: High heat

Shrimp:

3   pounds uncooked large shrimp, peeled and de-veined, tails left intact
      (can use cooked, frozen shrimp)

1. Bring large pot of water to a boil.
2. Add shrimp and cook until pink and opaque. Approximately 3 minutes.
3. Using a slotted spoon, transfer shrimp to a large bowl of ice water. Drain and place shrimp in a large bowl.

Chile Pepper Marinade:

¾	cup olive oil	¼	teaspoon cayenne pepper
½	cup cilantro, finely chopped	1	lemon, sliced
¼	cup white wine vinegar	3	large red onions, chopped
3	tablespoons fresh lemon juice	½	red pepper, chopped
2	jalapeño peppers, ribbed, seeded and minced	½	yellow pepper, chopped
4	large garlic cloves, minced		

1. Whisk oil, cilantro, vinegar, lemon juice, jalapeños, cloves and cayenne pepper in a medium bowl to blend. (Note: reduce spiciness by reducing cayenne pepper and jalapeño peppers.)
2. Season with salt and pepper.
3. Pour marinade over shrimp and toss to coat.
4. Layer shrimp, lemon slices, onion and peppers in a large glass bowl and pour any remaining marinade over.
5. Cover and refrigerate 4 hours.
6. Can be prepared a full day ahead. Keep shrimp refrigerated.
7. Optional: The shrimp and marinade can be served with cold cooked rice for a summer salad.

Yield: 12 servings

Jalapeño Pistachios

Prep time: 10 Minutes
Cook time: Overnight
Oven: 250 degrees

1   26 ounce can of jalapeños
1   teaspoon of garlic powder
4   pounds pistachios, shelled and roasted

1. Blend jalapeños and garlic powder in a blender or food processor.
2. Pour pistachios and jalapeño mix in a roasting pan and combine.
3. Place in oven at 250 degrees and stir every 60 minutes until dry.
4. Leave in the oven overnight or for 8 hours at 175 degrees.
5. Serve in party bowl.
6. Freeze unused pistachios for next party!

Yield: 20 servings

Fiesta Bowl Chicken Soup

Prep time: 10 minutes
Cook time: 10 minutes
Simmer: Low heat

Soup:

12   ounces salsa verde
3   cups chicken, cooked and diced
15   ounces cannelloni beans, drained
3   cups chicken broth
1   teaspoon ground cumin
2   green onions, chopped
½   cup sour cream
        tortilla chips (optional)

1.   Pour the salsa verde into sauce pan.
2.   Heat for two minutes over medium heat.
3.   Add chicken, beans and broth. Double the chicken broth for a lighter consistency.
4.   Bring to a boil and lower heat to simmer and cook for 10 minutes.
5.   Top each bowl with a sprinkling of onions, a dollop of sour cream and some tortilla chips.

Note: To make less spicy, use mild salsa verde and add to taste.

Yield: 6 Servings

Mixed Greens with Candied Walnuts, Goat Cheese and Kiwi

Caramelized Walnuts

Prep time: 5 minutes
Cook time: 5-6 minutes

½   cup walnut halves   2   teaspoons sugar
1   tablespoon water   2   teaspoons butter

1. In small saucepan, combine walnut halves with water, sugar and butter.
2. Cook over medium heat, stirring occasionally to coat nuts, approximately 5-6 minutes or until walnuts are toasted and glaze is caramel in color.
3. Place hot nuts on a sheet of foil to cool.

Hazelnut Vinaigrette Dressing

Prep time: 10 minutes

2 tablespoons fresh basil, minced	½ cup olive oil
2 tablespoons fresh parsley, minced	6 tablespoons rice vinegar
1½ teaspoons garlic, minced or pressed	6 tablespoons hazelnut oil
1½ teaspoons Dijon mustard	

1. Mix minced fresh basil, parsley, garlic and mustard in medium bowl.
2. Gradually whisk in olive oil, rice vinegar and hazelnut oil.
3. Season dressing to taste with salt and pepper.

Yield: 1½ cups

Salad

Prep time: 10 minutes

8 cups mixed salad greens	¼ cup small red onion,
6 ounces baby kiwi	cut into thin slivers
1 avocado, peeled and sliced	1 package crumbled goat cheese
	½ cup hazelnut vinaigrette

1. Place clean salad greens in a large bowl.
2. Arrange a mound of baby kiwi in the middle, and fan sliced avocado and red onion around kiwi. Sprinkle salad with goat cheese and caramelized walnuts; chill. Toss with hazelnut vinaigrette (or vinaigrette of your choice) just before serving.

The Portland Saturday Market

Any first visit to Portland must include a trip to the Portland Saturday Market. Situated in the oldest section of downtown near the waterfront, this market hosts local artisans, entertainers and international food vendors each weekend from March to December.

This market is a colorful way to spend an afternoon searching for locally made gifts or just browsing and grabbing a plate for lunch while enjoying a band. Artisans sell diverse products from candles and jewelry to hand-carved wood works and even jackets for pets.

Tarragon Roasted Potato Wedges

Prep time: 10 minutes
Bake time: 30 minutes
Oven: 425 degrees

Potatoes:

3   medium potatoes
¾   cup herb-seasoned stuffing mix, finely crushed
½   teaspoon fresh tarragon, finely chopped
½   teaspoon salt
⅛   teaspoon pepper
1   cup butter, melted

1.   Cut each potato lengthwise into 8 wedges.
2.   Combine stuffing with tarragon, salt, and pepper.
3.   Dip potato wedges into the melted butter then dredge in stuffing mixture and place on lightly greased jelly roll pan (15x10x1).
4.   Bake in oven 425 degrees for 30 minutes, or until potatoes are tender.

Yield: 4 servings

Blossom Festival Asparagus with Dijon Tarragon Vinaigrette

Prep time: 15 minutes

Asparagus:

2 pounds fresh asparagus

1. Steam asparagus until just tender.
2. Remove from steamer rack and refresh in ice water.

Dressing:

3 tablespoons boiling water
¼ cup Dijon mustard
⅓ cup olive oil
2 tablespoons rice vinegar
 salt and pepper to taste
2 tablespoons fresh tarragon, minced (or 1 1/2 tablespoons dried tarragon)

1. Slowly whisk the water into the mustard with a wire whisk.
2. Slowly whisk in the olive oil until it forms a thick, creamy sauce.
3. Add vinegar a little at a time until pleasantly tart.
4. Season with salt, fresh ground pepper and tarragon.
5. Place chilled asparagus on a platter and drizzle the vinaigrette lightly over the top.
6. Serve with extra vinaigrette on side.

Yield: 8 servings

Hood River Valley Blossom Festival

More than 15,000 acres of pear trees burst into pink and white blossoms every April at the Hood River Valley Blossom Festival. Visitors flock to enjoy the scenery and wafts of spring air in the Hood River Valley, located just over an hour east of Portland. The event, organized by the Hood River County Chamber of Commerce, includes a 45-mile driving tour around the valley where farmers along the route offer special blossom-time activities during the weekend. The Blossom Festival is a great way for out-of-town guests to catch a glimpse of easygoing farm country at the foot of the Cascades.

Grilled Corn with Serrano Lime Butter

Prep time: 15 minutes
Cook time: 20 minutes
Grill: medium

Corn:

4 ears of corn
1-2 serrano chiles, seeds and ribs removed and finely diced
¼ cup melted butter
½ fresh lime, juice
salt and pepper to taste

1. Shuck corn.
2. Melt butter in rectangular pan that you can roll corn in.
3. Add chiles, lime juice, salt and pepper.
4. Roll corn in butter sauce, salt and pepper to taste.
5. Individually wrap each piece of corn in aluminum foil.
6. Grill on medium temperature for 20 minutes, rolling over to other side after 10 minutes.

Yield: 4 servings

Cinco de Mayo Cilantro Grilled Chicken

Prep time: 20 minutes
Marinate: 1 hour
Cook time: 12-16 minutes

Chicken:

4   chicken breasts, boned and skinned (½ pound each)

Marinade:

⅓   cup olive oil
2   limes, juice
¼   cup balsamic vinegar
1   teaspoon Dijon mustard
2   cloves of garlic, minced
2   tablespoons cilantro, chopped
½   teaspoon seasoned salt
½   teaspoon coarse ground black pepper

1. Pound chicken breasts between waxed paper enough to flatten.
2. Combine oil, lime juice, balsamic vinegar, Dijon mustard, garlic, cilantro, salt and pepper in a bowl.
3. Add chicken and marinate for at least one hour.
3. Grill or broil chicken breasts for 6 to 8 minutes on each side, basting once.

Yield: 4 servings

Cinco de Mayo

Each year the Portland-Guadalajara Sister City Association presents Portland's Cinco de Mayo fiesta. The waterfront fills with Central American food vendors, entertainers from Guadalajara and Oregon and a huge carnival. Local and Hispanic-based artisans sell wares in a huge tent while kids can take part in their own cultural activities.

Skewered Beef with Snake River Onion Salsa

Prep time: 30 minutes
Marinate time: Overnight
Cook time: 5-8 minutes

Skewered Beef

16 ounces tender steak such as a New York Strip (top sirloin also works)
½   teaspoon ground cumin
½   teaspoon cardamom
1   teaspoon paprika
¼   teaspoon salt
¼   teaspoon pepper
½   teaspoon garlic powder
2   garlic cloves, minced
1   tablespoon olive oil

1. Cut beef into cubes.
2. Place beef in bowl with cumin, cardamom, paprika, salt, pepper, garlic powder, garlic and olive oil.
3. Toss well, cover and refrigerate overnight.
4. Spear cubes of beef onto skewers. (Don't pack too tightly. If using wooden skewers, soak them in water for 30 minutes before using.)
5. Cook the skewered beef on a grill or broil for about 5-8 minutes, or until the meat is well browned, but a little pink inside.
6. Serve hot with the Snake River salsa.

Snake River Salsa

½   red onion, finely diced
2   large Roma tomatoes, seeded and chopped
2   tablespoons red wine vinegar
¼   mint leaves, finely chopped

1. Combine red onion, tomatoes, vinegar, and mint leaves and place in refrigerator until ready to serve.

Yield: 4 servings

GRANDE RONDE RIVER
ROASTED LAMB

Prep time: 10 minutes
Marinate time: 10 to 12 hours
Cook time: 1 1/2 hours
Resting time: 15 minutes
Oven: 350 degrees

LAMB:

3-4   pounds leg of domestic lamb

MARINADE:

3   cloves garlic, minced
1½   inches of ginger root, peeled
½   bunch cilantro, lightly chopped
½   teaspoon pepper
¼   cup soy sauce
¼   cup Worcestershire sauce
¼   cup sherry
1   lemon, juice
2   teaspoons cumin
2   tablespoons Dijon mustard
¼   cup walnut oil
¼   cup olive oil

1. Mix garlic, ginger, cilantro, pepper, soy sauce, Worcestershire sauce, sherry, lemon juice, cumin, Dijon mustard, walnut oil and olive oil together in a bowl.
2. Pour over leg of lamb.
3. Marinate in refrigerator for 10 to 12 hours.
4. Roast in oven at 350 degrees until meat thermometer registers 140 degrees (rare). Approximately 1 ½ hours.
5. Remove roast from oven and let stand for 15 minutes. (Internal temperature will rise to medium rare.)
6. Slice and serve. Decorate serving platter with cilantro.

Yield: 6-8 Servings.

Oregon Trail

Over 150 years ago, eager pioneers set out from Independence, Missouri each spring for an epic journey across Kansas, Nebraska, Wyoming, Idaho and Oregon. They risked great hardship to stake their claim for a better life along the historic Oregon Trail.

Starting at the Oregon-Idaho border the Trail crosses the Snake River south of Nyssa and goes through Keeney Pass where deep wagon ruts are still visible. The route continues to the Malheur River and into Vale. The Stone House there was built in 1872 and served as a hotel, post office and store. At Farewell Bend State Park emigrants left the Snake River, pulling up the first of many long hills and ascending the dreaded Burnt River Canyon.

The National Historic Oregon Trail Interpretive Center at Baker City and Flagstaff Hill recreates life along the Trail. The nearby Hells Canyon Scenic Byway offers views of world's deepest river gorge.

Hells Canyon Fish Tacos with Guacamole and Corn Salsa

Prep time: 30 minutes
Cook time: 20 minutes
Oven: Broil

Tacos:

4   tablespoons salted butter, room temperature
½   fresh jalapeño pepper, ribbed, seeded and chopped
2   tablespoons cilantro, chopped
½   lime, juice
        salt to taste
2   pounds halibut filets or other white fish, such as tilapia
8   corn tortillas
        lime wedges

1.   Preheat oven to broil.
2.   With a fork, mix softened butter, jalapeño, cilantro and lime juice.
3.   Lightly salt fish filets and then cover with butter mixture.
4.   Squeeze lime juice over fish and broil for 20 minutes. (Fish can also be grilled, but must be brushed with butter mixture during cooking.)
5.   Serve fish with tortillas and lime wedges. Top with guacamole and corn salsa.

Guacamole:

3   medium or 2 large ripe avocados
¼   small red onion, diced
2   cloves garlic, minced
1½   teaspoon seasoned salt
1   fresh jalapeño, finely diced
1   pickled jalapeño, finely diced
1   tablespoon juice from jar of pickled jalapeños
¼   cup of fresh cilantro, coarsely chopped
1   lime, juice

1. Gently mash avocados with fork or potato masher.
2. Add red onion, garlic, salt, fresh and pickled jalapeños, jalapeño juice, cilantro and lime juice. Mix until well combined.
3. Guacamole can be made up to a day in advance. To prevent browning, press plastic wrap firmly onto surface of dip and refrigerate.

Note: These proportions will make spicy dip. If you want it milder or spicier, add more or less of the jalapeños and jalapeño juice. Tip: for less spicy remove the seeds and ribs of the jalapeños.

Corn Salsa:

2   cups corn
2   cups black or kidney beans
¼   cup cilantro, chopped
½   fresh jalapeño, ribbed, seeded and diced
½   cup cheddar cheese
2   teaspoons salt
2   tablespoons rice vinegar
½   lime juice

1. Mix corn , beans , cilantro , jalapeño, cheese, salt vinegar, and lime juice.
2. Refrigerate until ready to serve.

Yield: 4-8 servings

In the Grande Ronde Valley near LaGrande, known to the Native Americans as "The Valley of Peace" pioneers continued to the Blue Mountain where they welcomed the shade of pine and fir trees, but cursed the rocks. From the Blue Mountains the Trail winds through the Umatilla Valley into Pendleton, and west to Echo, crossing the Umatilla River at Fort Henrietta Park.

Next, the pioneers crossed the Deschutes River and reached The Dalles. Here, emigrants chose between rafting down the Columbia or taking the rugged Barlow Road route around Mt. Hood. Choosing the river route, pioneers next landed in Hood River, and the Cascade Locks where they were forced to leave the river and portage their goods, around the rough rapids. Finally, river travelers arrived at Fort Vancouver, where they crossed the river to travel overland into Oregon City.

Those who chose the Barlow Road route, which was forged by Samuel Barlow and Joel Palmer in 1845, went around Mt. Hood. As pioneers traveled on to Oregon City they passed by the Baker Cabin near Carver, the only cantilevered pioneer log cabin in Oregon. Finally, after traveling nearly 2000 miles, in five months, the pioneers entered Oregon City, and found the end of the Trail at Abernethy Green.

Sellwood Black Bean Lasagna

Prep time: 30 minutes
Cook time: 45 minutes
Oven: 350 degrees

Lasagna:

1	package lasagna noodles
4	jalapeño peppers, seeded, ribs removed and chopped
2	cups onions, chopped
2	cups bell pepper, chopped
4	garlic cloves, diced
1	12 ounce can diced tomatoes, drained
½	teaspoon cinnamon
2	14½ ounce cans black beans, drained
3	tablespoons cilantro, chopped
1	8 ounce carton low fat sour cream
3	cups salsa
1	16 ounce package Monterey Jack cheese, shredded

1. Cook the lasagna noodles until al dente.
2. In a large saucepan combine jalapeño peppers, onions, bell peppers and garlic and sauté for 5 minutes until onions are soft.
3. Add tomatoes and cinnamon and cook for 3 minutes.
4. Add black beans and cook for 3 minutes.
5. Remove pan from heat and cool for 5 minutes.
6. Add cilantro and sour cream. Mix well.
7. In lasagna pan, spread layer of salsa on bottom. Layer noodles, top with bean mixture, layer of cheese, layer of salsa. Continue until pan is full.
8. Top with cheese.
9. Tent with foil and bake covered in oven 350 degrees for 30 minutes.
10. Uncover and bake an additional 15 minutes.

Yield: 6 servings

Grilled Scallop Salad

Prep time: 20 minutes
Cook time: 20 minutes

Asparagus:

24   asparagus spears, trimmed

1.   In a large saucepan, bring 6 cups water to a boil. Add asparagus, cover and boil for 3 minutes.
2.   Drain and place asparagus in ice water. Pat dry and set aside.

Scallops and Mushrooms:

2   tablespoons olive oil
1   teaspoon soy sauce
24   sea scallops
2   cups fresh mushrooms, sliced
     cooking spray

1.   In a large zip bag, combine oil and soy sauce; add scallops.
2.   Seal bag and turn to coat. Let stand for 10 minutes.
3.   Arrange mushrooms on a 9 inch square piece of heavy duty foil coated with cooking spray.
4.   Grill mushrooms on foil uncovered over medium heat for 10-15 minutes or until tender, stirring often.
5.   Coat grill rack with non-stick cooking spray.
6.   Grill scallops, uncovered, over medium heat for 7-8 minutes on each side or until the scallops are firm and opaque.

Salad:

2   cups Boston lettuce, torn
¼   cup bacon, cooked and crumbled
1   cup walnuts, toasted and chopped
2   tablespoons Romano cheese, grated
     deli balsamic vinaigrette salad dressing to taste

1.   Arrange lettuce on four serving plates. Top with asparagus, scallops, mushrooms, bacon, walnuts and cheese.
2.   Drizzle with dressing.

Yield: 4 servings

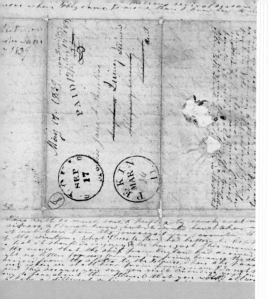

The Narcissus Whitman Papers: A Chronicle of Pioneer Sacrifice

In 1954, the Junior League of Portland out-bid several potential buyers for a dramatic piece of Oregon history and purchased the Narcissus Whitman papers for the Oregon Historical Society. These writings document the long journey over the Oregon Trail to the Blue Mountains in Eastern Oregon where missionary pioneers Narcissus Whitman and her husband, Marcus founded a mission that for five years, provided food, medical attention, and blacksmithing services. Following the November 29, 1847, murders of the Whitmans, the mission closed down and was bypassed, shaving a few miles off the journey.

The Whitman's were early pioneers to cross the Oregon Trail and Narcissus' writings detail the routes they took, the dramatic events that led up to their murders by Cayuse Indians and provided insight into which routes were better to travel on for future pioneers.

Silver Falls Chicken and Lime Salad

Prep time:	20 minutes
Marinate time:	1 hour
Cook time:	20 minutes

Chicken Marinade:

1	lime, juice
¼	cup salad oil
1	teaspoon cumin
4	medium size boneless, skinless chicken breasts (2 whole chicken breasts, cut in half)

1. Combine lime juice, oil and cumin and brush over chicken.
2. Marinate chicken for 1 hour.
3. Grill or broil chicken on medium heat until cooked. Approximately 20 minutes.

Dressing:

1	tablespoon garlic, minced
1	cup honey
1	tablespoon dry mustard
1	tablespoon white pepper
2	tablespoons sugar
1	tablespoon cumin
2	teaspoons chili powder
¼	teaspoon cayenne
⅓	cup fresh lime juice
¼	cup orange juice
1	cup cider vinegar
3	cups vegetable oil
½	tablespoon cilantro, minced (optional)
¼	small onion, chopped

1. Combine garlic, honey, mustard, pepper, sugar, cumin, chili powder, cayenne, lime juice, orange juice, vinegar, oil, cilantro and onion and set aside.

SALAD:

1   head romaine lettuce, chopped
    red onion to taste, thinly sliced
1   avocado, chopped
1   cup artichoke hearts, chopped

1. Combine lettuce, onion, avocado and artichoke hearts.
2. Toss with dressing.
3. Slice chicken breasts and arrange on top of salad and serve.

Yield: 4 servings (dressing is enough for 3-4 servings of 4. Saves for 2-3 weeks.)

WILLAMETTE VALLEY CRISP

Prep time: 10 minutes
Cook time: 30 minutes
Preheat: Oven 375 degrees (Place oven rack in center position)

CRISP:

4   cups fresh or 1, 16 ounce frozen tart berries (only use one kind of berry)
1   tablespoon lemon juice
½   cup flour
1   cup light brown sugar, firmly packed
½   teaspoon ground cinnamon
¼   cup unsalted butter, softened and cut into pieces
¾   cup rolled oats
    butter-flavored cooking spray

1. Lightly spray 1½ quart shallow baking dish with butter-flavored cooking spray.
2. Spread the berries evenly over bottom of dish and sprinkle with the lemon juice.
3. In a separate bowl, mix flour, sugar, cinnamon, butter and oats together with a fork until well combined.
4. Sprinkle evenly over berries.
5. Bake until top is golden and berries are bubbling. Approximately 30 minutes.

Yield: 6 servings

Double Chocolate Cherry Drops

Prep time: 15 minutes
Cook time: 10-12 minutes
Oven: 350 degrees

Drops:

1½   cups flour
½   teaspoon baking soda
½   teaspoon salt
⅔   cups brown sugar, firmly packed
½   cup butter
1   egg, beaten
¼   cup maraschino cherry juice
2   tablespoons milk
2   squares (2 ounces) unsweetened chocolate, melted
½   cup walnuts, chopped
¼   cup maraschino cherries, chopped
1   cup semi-sweet chocolate pieces

1. Sift together flour, baking soda and salt and set aside.
2. Cream together brown sugar and butter.
3. Add egg, ¼ of the dry ingredients, cherry juice and milk.
4. Stir in remaining dry ingredients.
5. Blend in unsweetened chocolate, walnuts, cherries and chocolate pieces.
6. Drop by round teaspoon onto a baking sheet.
7. Bake at 350 degrees for 10-12 minutes.
8. Optional-Frost with your favorite chocolate frosting.

Yield: 3 dozen.

Rosebuds in Bloom

Sunriver Soiree

Rose Garden Iced Wine

Baked Brie Quesadillas *with Mango and Avocado Salsa*

Peach and Tomato Salad *with Cilantro Lime Vinaigrette*

Columbia River Grilled Salmon *with Blueberry Sauce*

Blackberry Ice Cream Pie

Oregonians love nature and in the summer they live outdoors! They get away to the beach or mountain resorts like Sunriver to enjoy outdoor pursuits and to relax. Elegant, but casual entertaining is the norm and whether at the mountains, the beach or in town, Oregonians find many occasions to celebrate the summer.

Portland, Oregon's largest city, is home to one of the world's most famous rose gardens, the International Rose Test Garden. Each year hundreds of thousands of visitors from around the world visit this garden. Many consider the Garden Portland's signature landmark which also boasts spectacular city views among more than 8,000 roses.

The Rose Garden is the oldest continuously operated public rose test garden in the United States. In 1917, three prominent nurserymen met in Portland and decided a spot high in the hills above the city was the perfect location for an American test garden. Back then, Portland claimed over 200 miles of rose-bordered streets and had already been dubbed "City of Roses." The Rose Garden seemed like icing on the cake.

Today, locals visit the garden on summer evenings to take in concerts at the Rose Garden's amphitheater, have a picnic or just read a book on a park bench and breathe in the heavily scented air.

The Waterfront Blues Festival

Portland is home to the largest blues festival west of the Mississippi which brings in more than 120,000 visitors every Fourth of July weekend. The waterfront is absolutely packed to the brim when acts like Buddy Guy and Mavis Staples come to Portland.

The Festival also offers blues cruises, where festival goers can buy tickets to an up-close-and-personal performance with festival acts and cruise the Willamette River on the Portland Spirit.

Baked Brie Quesadillas with Mango & Avocado Salsa

Prep time: 30 minutes
Cook time: 5 minutes
Oven: 350 degrees

Salsa:

2   avocados, peeled, pitted, diced in ½ inch cubes
3   small mangos, peeled, pitted, diced in ½ inch cubes
1   teaspoon each red and green pepper, finely diced
1   tablespoon green onion, finely diced
1   teaspoon fresh lime juice
3   tablespoons olive oil
1   teaspoon cilantro, chopped
1   serrano chile, seeded, ribbed and finely diced
    salt to taste

1. Combine avocado, ½ of mango cubes, peppers and green onions in a mixing bowl.
2. Pour lime juice, olive oil, cilantro, serrano chile and remaining mango cubes in blender and puree for 30 seconds.
3. Drizzle over avocado mixture.
4. Season with salt and toss gently.

Quesadillas:

1   small wheel of Brie cheese
12 flour tortillas

1. Slice Brie into ½ inch thick slices.
2. Top half of each tortilla with ½ inch thick slices of firm Brie or spread a thick layer of soft Brie; fold in half.
3. Lightly coat tops of tortillas with cooking spray. Bake at 350 degrees for 5 minutes or until cheese is melted and tortillas begin to brown.
4. Cut each tortilla into 3 wedges and top with a dollop of salsa.

Yield: 12 servings

Rose Garden Iced Wine

Prep time: 24 hours

Equal parts:
White wine
Club soda
Lemonade concentrate, do not add water
Sprig of mint or rosemary for garnish, optional

Mixing:
1.   Mix equal parts white wine, club soda, and lemonade concentrate.
2.   Cover and freeze for 24 hours.
3.   To serve, scoop frozen mixture into glasses. Garnish with optional sprig of mint or rosemary.

Yield: 4-6 servings.

Peach and Tomato Salad with Cilantro Lime Vinaigrette

Prep time: 20 minutes

Vinaigrette:

3   tablespoons extra-virgin olive oil
1   tablespoon balsamic vinegar
1   tablespoon fresh lime juice
1   teaspoon salt
½   teaspoon black pepper, freshly ground

1. Whisk together olive oil, vinegar, lime juice, ½ teaspoon salt, and ¼ teaspoon pepper in a small bowl; set vinaigrette aside.

Salad:

4   large, peaches
3   large red heirloom tomatoes
1½   cups cherry tomatoes, halved
2   small celery stalks cut into ½ inch pieces
¼   cup fresh cilantro leaves, plus sprigs for garnish

1. Halve and pit peaches. Cut halves into quarters. Remove core from stem end of large tomatoes; slice into ½ inch rounds.
2. Arrange peaches, tomatoes, cherry tomatoes, and celery on a serving plate. Sprinkle with remaining ¼ teaspoon salt and pepper. Coarsely chop cilantro leaves; add to vinaigrette.
3. Pour over salad, and garnish with cilantro sprigs.

Yield: 8 to 10 servings

CRATER LAKE COLESLAW

Prep time: Cabbage-10 minutes
                Dressing-10 minutes
Marinate: Overnight or 6-8 hours

COLESLAW:

3   cups green cabbage, peeled and shredded
3   cups red cabbage, peeled and shredded
2   carrots, peeled and shredded
½   green pepper, chopped
½   medium red onion, peeled and chopped
½   cup sugar

1. In a bowl combine the cabbage, carrots, green pepper and onion.
2. Sprinkle with sugar.

DRESSING:

2   teaspoons sugar
1   cup rice vinegar
1   teaspoon celery seed
¾   cup vegetable oil
1   teaspoon dry yellow mustard
1   teaspoon salt
1   teaspoon black pepper

1. In a saucepan, combine sugar, vinegar, celery seed, oil, dry mustard, salt, pepper. Stir until well blended and bring to a boil.
2. Pour over the vegetables, stirring to cover evenly.
3. Cover and refrigerate overnight or for 6-8 hours.
4. Stir well before serving.

Yield: 6 servings

THE BITE OF OREGON

The Bite may appear to be just another waterfront gathering, but don't let it fool you. Organizers tout the Bite as, "The premier showcase of Oregon Food and Beverage." That means local Oregon ingredients are whipped up into fantastic plates by some of the areas most accomplished chefs and served alongside lauded Oregon beer and wine.

Join the masses of foodies in the warm weather of mid-August every year to not only enjoy food and beverages, but also see over 100 national and regional musical and comedy acts.

MARINATED ARTICHOKE AND POTATO SALAD

Prep time: 10 minutes
Cook time: 20 minutes

SALAD:

3	pounds even-sized potatoes, quartered
3	cups fresh green beans, washed and trimmed, cut into bite size pieces
1	(6-ounce) jar marinated artichoke hearts, un-drained
½	cup Kalamata olives, quartered
¼	cup fresh basil and flat-leaf parsley combined, and chopped
3	tablespoon white wine vinegar
½	teaspoon sugar
½	teaspoon freshly ground pepper
¼	teaspoon salt

1. Place potatoes in a large saucepan; cover with water. Bring to a boil, reduce heat and cook until just tender when pierced with a knife, about 15 minutes.
2. Add beans to potatoes and cook until beans are crisp-tender, about 2 minutes. Drain in a colander, rinse with cool water and cool to room temperature.
3. Cut potatoes into quarters and place in large bowl with beans.
4. Drain artichokes, reserving marinade. Chop artichokes and add artichokes and olives to the potatoes.
5. Mix reserved marinade with basil, parsley, vinegar, sugar, pepper and salt.
6. Add marinade to potato mixture, and toss to coat. Cover and chill.

Yield: 10 to 12 servings

Sun Kissed Potatoes with Saffron

Prep time: 15 minutes
Cook time: 1 hour
Oven: 350 degrees

Potatoes:

2   pounds baking potatoes, peeled and cubed, approximately 2 large potatoes
½   cup yellow onion, finely chopped
½   cup leek, finely chopped
3   tablespoons butter
1   tablespoon lemon peel, grated
3   tablespoons fresh lemon juice
½   teaspoon salt
¼   teaspoon pepper
2   tablespoons saffron

1. Cook potatoes in boiling water to cover for 15 minutes or microwave until tender; set aside.
2. Sauté chopped onion and leek in melted butter in a large skillet over medium heat until tender.
3. Add lemon peel, lemon juice, salt, and pepper, and stir well.
4. Add potatoes, and stir gently to combine.
5. Spoon potato mixture into a lightly greased 11 x 7 baking dish.
6. Bake, uncovered, at 350 degrees for 15 minutes.
7. Broil, uncovered, at 350 degrees for 10 minutes or until potatoes are golden brown.
8. Sprinkle with saffron and serve.

Yield: 6 servings

The International Pinot Noir Celebration

A writer from the Chicago Tribune called this event "The Woodstock of Wine." Each year, the International Pinot Noir Celebration invades the small wine country town of McMinnville. It is the self-proclaimed, small summer camp-like experience for wine industry types and simple consumers alike.

Attendance is by reservation only to keep the celebration casual while participants sip libations with 60 top pinot noir makers from Oregon and around the world. Oregon wine makers play "camp counselor" and take visitors on wine country tours, tastings, lectures, viticulture seminars and fabulous dinners with some of Oregon's most celebrated chefs.

COLUMBIA RIVER GRILLED SALMON WITH BLUEBERRY SALSA

Prep time: 20 minutes
Cook time: 10-15 minutes

SALSA:

1	cup blueberries, coarsely chopped
½	cup orange, peeled and coarsely chopped
¼	cup red pepper, minced
¼	cup green pepper, minced
¼	cup red onion, minced
¼	cup cilantro, chopped
¼	cup mint, chopped
1	tablespoon fresh lime juice
½	teaspoon lime peel, grated
2	teaspoons jalapeño pepper, seeded, ribbed and minced
	salt and pepper to taste

1. In a small bowl, combine blueberries, orange, red pepper, green pepper, red onion, cilantro, mint, lime juice, lime peel, jalapeño, and salt to taste.
2. Allow to stand 1-2 hours at room temperature.

SALMON:

6	salmon fillets, skin removed
4	tablespoon butter
¼	cup pinot noir
2	tablespoon brown sugar, firmly packed
	salt and pepper to taste

1. Heat butter, wine and brown sugar in small saucepan over medium heat until melted and slightly reduced.
2. Brush on both sides of salmon and season with salt and pepper.
3. Grill on barbecue for 5-7 minutes each side and baste with wine sauce during cooking.
4. Serve topped with blueberry salsa.

Yields: 6 servings

Herb Grilled Halibut for a Midsummer Night

Prep time: 20 minutes
Marinate: 1 hour
Cook time: 6-8 minutes
Grill: Medium heat

Halibut:

3   tablespoons white wine
3   tablespoons olive oil
3   tablespoons fresh lemon juice
2   tablespoons fresh rosemary, chopped
4   halibut steaks
    salt and pepper to taste
1   lemon, sliced for garnish

1. Whisk together wine, oil and lemon juice and ½ fresh chopped rosemary in a small shallow baking dish.
2. Add halibut and turn to coat. Marinate in the refrigerator for 1 hour, turning once.
3. Remove fish from marinade and season with salt and pepper to taste.
4. Grill for 3-4 minutes on each side.
5. Garnish with other ½ fresh chopped rosemary and lemon slices.

Yields: 4 servings

Marinated Turkey Tenderloin Skewers with Peanut Sauce

Prep time: 20 minutes
Marinate: 4 hours
Cook time: 20 minutes

Turkey:

2   pounds turkey breast tenderloins cut into small cubes, about 1½ inches

Marinade:

½   cup dry sherry
¼   cup olive oil
¼   cup lite soy sauce
9   garlic cloves, minced
1   tablespoon sugar
½   teaspoon ground black pepper

1. Combine sherry, olive oil, soy sauce, garlic, sugar and black pepper in large bowl.
2. Add turkey and toss to coat. Cover and refrigerate at least 4 hours, can be marinated all day or overnight.
3. Thread turkey onto skewers and cook over direct heat on grill, turning frequently, brushing with remaining marinade until turkey is not pink in the center, about 20 minutes.

Peanut Sauce:

1   teaspoon cornstarch
½   cup water
⅓   cup lite soy sauce
½   cup smooth peanut butter
¼   cup sesame oil
1   teaspoon red pepper flakes (optional)
2   tablespoons sugar
¼   teaspoon hot chile oil (optional)
¼   cup fresh cilantro, chopped
¼   cup green onions, chopped

1. In saucepan, stir cornstarch in water until starch dissolves.
2. Add soy sauce, peanut butter, sesame oil, red pepper flakes, sugar, hot chile oil, and mix until smooth.
3. Bring sauce to a boil over medium-high heat, stirring frequently.
4. Reduce heat to low and simmer about 5 minutes until sauce thickens.
5. Let cool and stir in cilantro and onions.
6. Serve peanut sauce warm for dipping turkey or spread over rice and turkey.

Note: Sauce can be made 3 days in advance and refrigerated or frozen for up to 1 month.

Yields: 4 servings

Cannon Beach Beer Can Chicken

Prep time: 1 hour 15 minutes
Cook time: 3 hours
Grill: Low heat (225-275 degrees)

Chicken:
1   whole chicken
¼   cup dry rub of your choice
1   12 ounce can of beer
3   cups Italian dressing

1. Remove giblets and rinse inside of chicken.
2. Season the chicken inside and out with the dry rub. Let sit for 1 hour.
3. Open can of beer and drink or pour half of it out.
4. Refill can with Italian dressing.
5. Roll chicken in Italian dressing so that it is thoroughly coated.
6. Set can upright on grill and set chicken cavity over the can with chicken legs resting on top of grill.
7. Grill chicken on low heat 225 - 275 degrees for 3 hours, brushing the chicken with Italian dressing every hour.

Note: Place large aluminum roasting pan under grill to catch drippings. Discard drippings.

Yield: 4 servings

Burnside Baby Backs

Ribs:

Prep time: 5 minutes
Cook time: 2 hours
Oven: 350 degrees

Sauce:

Prep time: 10 minutes
Cook time: 30 minutes
Oven: 350 degrees

Ribs:

4   sides baby back pork ribs   salt and pepper to taste

1. Preheat oven to 350 degrees.
2. Place ribs meat side up on broiler pan.
3. Salt and pepper ribs.
4. Roast for 15 minutes, turn ribs over, roast another 15 minutes, cover with foil and continue roasting for 1 hour.
5. Prepare barbecue sauce.
6. After roasting ribs for 1 ½ hours, turn heat down to 300, turn ribs over so that meat side is up, and baste ribs with barbecue sauce.
7. Roast ribs for 15 minutes and baste with barbecue sauce again.
8. Roast for another 15 minutes.
9. Remove from oven, cut with knife or scissors between the ribs. Place on serving platter. Serve with remaining barbecue sauce.

Barbecue Sauce:

3 tablespoons butter	1 tablespoon cider vinegar
1 tablespoon garlic, minced	1 tablespoon dry yellow mustard
½ cup yellow onion, chopped	8 tablespoons fresh lemon juice
2 cups ketchup	¼ teaspoon ground cloves
½ cup brown sugar	½ teaspoon salt
½ cup Worcestershire sauce	½ teaspoon pepper
¼ cup chili sauce	

1. In a saucepan, melt butter, add garlic and onions. Sauté until onions are translucent.
2. Add ketchup, brown sugar, Worcestershire sauce, chili sauce, cider vinegar, dry mustard, lemon juice, cloves, salt, and pepper. Stir until all ingredients are blended.
3. Simmer slowly, on low heat for 30 minutes, stirring occasionally.
4. Place ½ cup of barbecue sauce in separate bowl to use for basting. Barbecue sauce may be made 2-3 days in advance and refrigerated, or 2 weeks in advance and frozen.

Yield: 6-8 servings

Apricot and Blueberry Chicken

Prep time: 20 minutes
Oven: 375 degrees
Cook time: 30 minutes

Chicken:

4	boneless, skinless chicken breast halves	1	cup dried apricots, chopped
1	cup apricot jam	1½	cups almonds, finely chopped
3	tablespoons Dijon mustard	¼	cup almond oil or olive oil
1	cup blueberries (fresh or frozen)		

1. In a small bowl, combine apricot jam and Dijon mustard. Set aside.
2. In another bowl, gently mix the blueberries and chopped apricots together. If using frozen blueberries do not thaw.
3. Using half of the blueberry/apricot mixture, spread over each of the chicken breasts and roll jelly-roll style.
4. Using half of the apricot jam/Dijon mustard mixture, cover each chicken roll with the mixture.
5. Roll each chicken roll in the fine chopped almonds to form a crust.
6. Cover and chill for 30 minutes and up to 4 hours. (Nuts will become soggy if you chill longer than 4 hours.)
7. Remove from the refrigerator and drizzle with oil. Bake at 375 degrees for 20 minutes. Tent chicken with foil to keep the nuts from browning.
8. Transfer the chicken breasts to a warm platter and cover with foil.

Sauce:

½   cup white wine vinegar
       reserved apricot/Dijon mustard spread
       reserved blueberry/apricot mixture

1. Add white wine vinegar to the pan and deglaze over high heat, loosening browned bits.
2. When liquid has reduced by half, turn burner to medium high and add the remaining half of the blueberry/apricot mixture and the apricot/Dijon mixture. Stir until bubbling.
3. Spoon sauce onto middle of four dinner plates and place one chicken breast on top of sauce on each plate. Garnish with blueberries and mint and serve immediately.

Yield: 4 servings

Fruit and Flower Shrimp and Pasta Salad

Prep time: 20 minutes
Cook time: 10 minutes

Salad:

1   pound small pasta, (penne, elbow, shells, fusilli)
3   cups small, bay shrimp
1   large fresh tomato, seeded and diced
¼   cup fresh parsley, chopped
3   tablespoons fresh basil, chopped
½   cup fresh dill, finely chopped
½   cup shallots, minced
3   tablespoons small capers
¼   cup Kalamata olives, chopped
½   cup lemon juice
2   tablespoons vegetable oil
1   tablespoon Dijon mustard
1   tablespoon white wine vinegar
½   cup olives, halved

1.   Cook pasta according to package directions. Drain.
2.   In a large bowl, combine pasta, shrimp, ½ cup tomatoes, parsley, basil, dill, shallots, capers, chopped olives and lemon juice. Add oil and toss.
3.   In a small bowl, mix mustard and vinegar until smooth.
4.   Pour over salad and toss well.
5.   Garnish with remaining tomatoes and halved olives.

Yield: 6 servings

Penne Pasta with Summer Asparagus and Sun-Dried Tomatoes

Prep time: 10 minutes
Cook time: 15 minutes

Salad:

4	tablespoons olive oil
1	pound fresh asparagus, cut into 1 inch pieces
¼	cup shallots or green onion, chopped
1	cup mushrooms, sliced
4	cloves garlic, chopped
¾	cup dry chardonnay wine
½	cup sun-dried tomatoes in oil, julienne cut
4	tablespoons chopped fresh basil
1	cup chicken stock
1	pound penne or other favorite pasta
	freshly grated Parmesan

1. Heat olive oil in skillet over medium heat.
2. Add asparagus, shallots or green onions, mushrooms, garlic and sauté briefly.
3. Add white wine and cook on high to reduce liquid.
4. Add sun-dried tomatoes, fresh basil, chicken stock and bring to a boil. Reduce heat and simmer 7-8 minutes.
5. Cook penne according to directions on package.
6. Combine asparagus mixture with cooked penne and sprinkle with fresh Parmesan.

Yield: 6-8 servings

Whitewater Rafting in Oregon

Even though Oregon has a breathtaking and extensive coastline, thrill seekers hit the state's rivers for bold whitewater action.

The Rogue River

The Rogue River running through Southwestern Oregon boasts challenging rapids but also allows plenty of time for swimming in its tepid waters or enjoying the abundant campsites. Watching for the region's wildlife and fishing for steelhead and salmon are common pastimes while boating the Rogue.

The Deschutes River

The Deschutes runs through Central Oregon, which enjoys an annual average of 300 days of sunshine per year. This river is divided into four segments with many different trips available. Novices and experts can find trips ranging from a one-hour paddle to a week long trip down the entire 100 miles. Much of the river has train tracks on one side and a primitive road on the other. However, there are still remote areas, great scenery and primitive riverside camps.

The McKenzie River

This Oregon gem is a classic alpine river high in the Cascade Range near Eugene in the Southern Willamette Valley. Cascading through a canyon lined with old growth forest, this river is considered an alpine jewel with an abundance of rapids. From picturesque waterfalls to stunning views of snow-capped mountains, this river is a fly-fishing and whitewater enthusiast's paradise.

Almond Cake with Strawberry Sauce

Cake:
Prep time: 10 minutes
Cook time: 40-50 minutes
Oven: 350 degrees

Sauce:
Prep time: 5 minutes
Cook time: 5 minutes
Oven: 350 degrees

Cake:

¾	cup sugar
½	cup unsalted butter, room temperature
8	ounces almond paste
3	eggs
1	tablespoon Amaretto
¼	teaspoon almond extract
¼	cup all-purpose flour
½	teaspoon baking powder
	powdered sugar

1. Combine sugar, butter and almond paste.
2. Beat in eggs, Amaretto, and almond extract.
3. Gently stir in flour and baking powder, mixing just until blended.
4. Pour batter into a greased and floured 8-inch round cake pan.
5. Bake at 350 degrees for 40 to 50 minutes, or until a wooden pick or cake tester inserted in center comes out clean.
6. Invert onto cake plate and sprinkle with powdered sugar. (Put powdered sugar into a sieve, hold over top of cake and tap sieve with knife to get a "snow covered" effect.)

Sauce:

2	cups fresh or frozen strawberries
⅓	cup sugar
1	tablespoon fresh lemon juice
¼	teaspoon salt
½	teaspoon vanilla extract

1. Wash and crush strawberries.
2. Add sugar, lemon juice and salt. Mix well.
3. In a small saucepan, bring strawberry mixture to a boil; boil 1 minute.
4. Add vanilla. Chill.
5. Spoon over cake.

Yield: Serves 6-8

Star Spangled Berry Pie

Prep time: 15 minutes
Chill time: 3 hours

Pie Shell:
1   9-inch pastry shell, baked

Berry Filling:
1½   cup raspberries
1½   cup strawberries, sliced
1   cup Marionberries
¾   cup sugar
3   tablespoons cornstarch
1½   cups water
1   0.6 ounce package strawberry gelatin
1   small carton heavy cream, whipped, with sugar and vanilla.

1.   Mix berries in large bowl.
3.   Mix sugar and cornstarch in medium sauce pan.
4.   Gradually stir in water until smooth. Cook on medium heat until mixture comes to a boil. Stir constantly. Boil 1 minute.
5.   Remove from heat and stir in gelatin until dissolved.
6.   Cool at room temperature.
7.   Pour mixture over berries, mix and pour into pastry shell.
8.   Refrigerate 3 hours.
9.   Serve with whipped cream.

Yield: 8 servings

The Mt. Hood Jazz Festival

Over the past 20 years, the Mt. Hood Festival has brought such national jazz figures as Sarah Vaughan, Dizzy Gillespie, Dave Brubeck, Wynton Marsalis, Ella Fitzgerald, Tony Bennett and George Benson to the Portland area. The festival also showcases emerging regional talent, which over time has included Tom Grant, Robert Cray, and Diane Schurr.

The festival has an intimate feel due to its location in the green environs of Gresham's Park, located in historic downtown Gresham just east of Portland. Acoustic jazz can easily be heard without a booming speaker system, so all spectators can savor the sounds. Food, microbrews, wines and picnic areas are also within reach.

BLACKBERRY ICE CREAM PIE

Prep time: 30 minutes
Bake time: 8 minutes
Chill time: 3 hours
Oven: 350 degrees

CRUST:
2   cups graham cracker crumbs
½   cup sugar
½   cup unsalted butter

1. Preheat oven to 350 degrees.
2. Place crackers in a food processor; process until fine crumbs form.
3. Add sugar and melted butter.
4. Pulse until moist.
5. Press crumb mixture into bottom and up sides of a 9-inch springform pan coated with cooking spray.
6. Bake at 350 degrees for 8 minutes.
7. Cool on a wire rack.
8. Freeze 30 minutes to overnight.

FILLING:
½   gallon softened premium vanilla ice cream
2   cups fresh or frozen, thawed blackberries

1. Scoop softened ice cream into pie shell and smooth to a flat surface.
2. Cover with plastic wrap and freeze at least 2 hours.

Sauce:

2   premium dark chocolate bars
½   cup unsalted butter

1. In a small saucepan, melt chocolate bars and butter together until smooth, stirring continuously.
2. Remove from heat and allow to cool at room temperature.

To Serve:

1. Place pie in refrigerator for 30 minutes before serving.
2. Before serving, gently mash 1 cup of blackberries and pour over pie.
3. Pour remaining whole berries on top.
4. Ladle several tablespoons of chocolate sauce onto bottom of each serving plate.
5. Place slice of pie on top of chocolate sauce.

Yield: 8-10 servings

᪥

The Harvest Moon

Golden Sunset Supper

Pacific Golden Chanterelle and Goat Cheese Crostini

Sauvie Island Tomato Soup *with Basil Cream*

Apple Stuffed Pork Loin *with Raspberry Sauce*

Chilled Apricot Torte

The harvest moon brings some of Oregon's finest weather along with a bountiful harvest, from our world famous wine grapes to vegetables and fall's bounty from the sea.

For Portlander's, the harvest moon also brings the season premier of bountiful cultural activities for which Portlanders are very proud. Celebrations honoring the big four abound this time of year as patrons gather to bring in the opening performances.

Portland Opera

For over 40 years, the Portland Opera has brought emotion-evoking performances to Oregon and has steadily gained national stature. With its commitment to producing operas that invigorate the future of the art form and are dramatically and vocally compelling, Portland Opera has developed a loyal following in the area.

Portland Art Museum

The Portland Art Museum is the oldest art museum in the Pacific Northwest and since its founding in 1892, has amassed a diverse collection of over 33,000 works of art. The Museum's collection comprises primarily gifts from donors and smaller collections purchased in their entirety.

Located in the Park Blocks of downtown Portland, the Museum's collection includes works of European painting and sculpture, American painting and sculpture, English silver, Asian art, Native American art, Pre-Columbian art, African art, contemporary art, sculpture, prints and drawings, and photography.

Oregon Symphony

Since the Oregon Symphony was established more than 100 years ago, it has been recognized for its internationally acclaimed music directors, skilled performers, diverse programs and unique community services and regional touring.

The Oregon Symphony now ranks among the largest orchestras in the nation and is one of the largest arts organizations in the Northwest. The organization also offers occasional outdoor concerts in the summer featuring tributes to contemporary and classical compositions.

Oregon Ballet Theatre

Oregon Ballet Theatre (OBT), established in August 1989, is the youngest of the "Big 4" in Portland. It is a classically-based professional ballet that offers an annual season of five productions including the annual holiday favorite, *The Nutcracker*.

Oregon Ballet Theatre's continuing goal is to provide its constituency with the finest in professional ballet performances, education, and training as Oregon's ambassador of dance.

Pacific Golden Chanterelle & Goat Cheese Crostini

Prep time: 10 minutes
Cook time: 10 minutes
Oven: 400 degrees

Crostini:

½   cup olive oil
1   baguette, sliced into 40 (¼-inch) thick slices

1. Preheat oven to 400 degrees.
2. Using a pastry brush, brush a cookie sheet with oil.
3. Place the sliced baguette on the cookie sheet and lightly brush each piece with oil.
4. Bake until golden brown on both sides.

Black Bean Puree:

1   cup black beans
½   cup extra-virgin olive oil
2   cloves of garlic
¼   cup fresh lemon juice
2   tablespoons grated Parmesan cheese
    dash of salt and pepper

1. Puree the black beans and extra-virgin olive oil, garlic, lemon juice, and Parmesan in a blender or food processor.
2. Season the mixture with salt and pepper.

Mushrooms:

1   cup fresh Chanterelle mushrooms, sliced into ¼-inch thick pieces
2   tablespoons minced shallots
2   tablespoons olive oil

1. In a skillet on high heat, sauté the mushrooms and shallots in 2 tablespoons olive oil until tender, season with salt and pepper to taste.

GOAT CHEESE:

½   cup fresh goat cheese

ASSEMBLY:

1.   Spread a spoonful of the black bean puree on each crostini and top with a small amount of goat cheese. Garnish with a piece of cooked chanterelle mushroom.

OREGON BLACKBERRY VODKA LEMONADE

Prep time:	5 minutes
Chilling time:	2 hours, or up to two days
Stovetop:	High flame

VODKA LEMONADE:

6	lemons
¾	cup chilled vodka
2	cups water
1	cup sugar
½	cup fresh blackberries
2	cups ice
	lemon slices for garnish

1.   With a vegetable peeler, remove zest from 4 lemons and squeeze enough juice from these and remaining 2 lemons to measure 1 cup.
2.   In a saucepan, boil 1 cup water with sugar, stirring until sugar is dissolved. Add zest, lemon juice and remaining 1 cup water. Allow to cool.
3.   In a food processor or blender, puree blackberries and stir into lemonade. Pour mixture through a sieve into a pitcher. Add vodka and chill, covered, at least 2 hours and up to 2 days.
4.   Serve over ice in a tall glass, and garnish with lemon slices.

Yield: 4 servings

OREGON BERRIES

Just south of Portland in Oregon's Willamette Valley, farmers produce some of the most notable berries in the world. Warm summer days and cold nights produce sweet and plump red raspberries, black raspberries, Marionberries, evergreen blackberries, boysenberries, and loganberries.

The Willamette Valley has long been considered to be berry paradise by fruit buyers and berry devotees worldwide, with over 50 varieties of berries cultivated for sale to worldwide markets. A unique maritime climate with long, mild spring weather allows Oregon berries to grow slowly, creating a tapestry of rich and intense flavor compounds.

Perhaps the most recognizable Oregon berry is the Marionberry. Grown exclusively in Oregon, the Marionberry was developed among the fields of Marion County as a cross between two varieties of blackberry. If you're in Portland and don't want to make the trek south to find Oregon berries, just follow Highway 30 to Sauvie Island where many local growers operate farmers markets or u-pick fields in the summer.

Sauvie Island Tomato Soup with Basil Cream

Prep time: 20 minutes
Cook time: 30 minutes
Stovetop: High flame

Soup:

2   tablespoons unsalted butter
4   large shallots, peeled and thinly sliced
2½   teaspoons of salt
3   pounds of tomatoes, peeled, seeded and chopped
1   pint chicken stock
½   cup heavy cream, chilled
½   cup loosely-packed fresh basil leaves, finely chopped
     whole basil leaves for garnish

1. Melt butter. Add shallots and sauté until wilted and lightly colored.
2. Stir in 2 teaspoons of salt and the tomatoes. Cover tightly and cook until tomatoes are soft.
3. Transfer the mixture to a food processor with a steel chopping blade and puree until smooth. Return puree to saucepan, stir in chicken stock and season with pepper.
4. Beat the heavy cream in a chilled bowl until it forms soft peaks. Stir in remaining salt and basil. Ladle the soup into bowls, add a dollop of the basil cream in the middle of each bowl and garnish with basil leaves.

Yield: 6 servings

Mixed Greens with Apples, Pears, Pecans and Poppy Seed Dressing

Prep time: 15 minutes

Dressing:
⅔   cup vegetable or canola oil
⅓   cup lemon juice
¼   cup sugar
2   teaspoons green onion, chopped
¾   teaspoon salt
1   teaspoon poppy seeds

1. Combine oil, lemon juice, sugar, green onion, salt and poppy seeds in a jar or container with tight fitting lid and shake well.

Salad:
8   cups mixed salad greens
1   medium sized semi-tart apple, coarsely chopped
1   medium pear, coarsely chopped
1   cup pecans, toasted and chopped
1   cup Swiss cheese, shredded
¼   cup dried cranberries

1. In a large bowl, combine greens, apple, pear, pecans, cheese and cranberries. Drizzle with dressing to taste and toss.
2. Serve Immediately.

Yield: 8 servings

Portland's Shanghai Tunnels

A series of dingy, creepy old tunnels still snake deep under the city streets, pubs and hotels of Portland. Why? In the mid-1800's when ship captains from around the world sailed into Portland, they were usually in the market for fresh crew members after a long journey.

A handful of crooked middlemen fulfilled this nautical need by drugging pub-goers and drunks upstairs in the bars and dropping them through trap doors in the floor. They carted them through the tunnels out to the waterfront. They then sold the incapacitated to captains at $50 a head. In the local vernacular of the time, this was called being "Shanghaied."

There are tours available to experience the tunnels, and many guides claim these depths to be haunted.

Belmont Couscous

Prep time: 20 minutes
Cook time: 30 minutes
Marinate: Overnight

Couscous:

4   cups chicken stock
6   tablespoons extra virgin olive oil
¼   teaspoon turmeric
¼   teaspoon cinnamon
¼   teaspoon ground ginger
2   cups couscous
½   cup currants
½   cup dates, chopped and pitted
2   cups zucchini-trimmed and coarsely chopped
1   cup carrots, peeled and coarsely chopped
1   large yellow onion, finely chopped
1½   tablespoons lemon juice, freshly squeezed
1   head leaf lettuce
½   cup slivered almonds, toasted
       salt and pepper to taste

1.   In a large saucepan, bring the chicken stock, 4 tablespoons olive oil, turmeric, cinnamon, and ground ginger to boil.
2.   Add the couscous and boil for 2 minutes.
3.   Remove from heat and fold in currants and dates.
4.   Cover tightly and let stand for 15 minutes.
5.   Add zucchini, carrots and onion; mix well.

Dressing:

1.   In a small bowl combine the lemon juice, 2 tablespoons olive oil, and salt and pepper.
2.   Pour dressing over the couscous.
3.   Toss to coat thoroughly, breaking up any clumps.
4.   Refrigerate overnight.
5.   To serve, arrange leaf lettuce on a large platter, cover with the couscous and sprinkle with the slivered almonds.

Yield: 6 servings

Central Oregon Beets in Orange Sauce

Prep time: 15 minutes
Cook time: 45 minutes

Beets:
8 beets, peeled, cooked and sliced
¼ cup yellow onion, grated
1 tablespoon red wine vinegar
3 tablespoons brown sugar
1 tablespoon melted butter
   juice and grated peel of 1 orange

1. Peel, slice and steam beets until tender.
2. Combine beets, onion, red wine vinegar, brown sugar, butter, orange juice and orange peel in a saucepan.
3. Cover tightly; bring to a boil. Reduce heat to medium-low; simmer for 10-15 minutes.

Yield: 4 servings

The Pendleton Round-Up

Following a July 4th celebration in 1909 consisting of bronc riding, horse races, Native American feasts and war dances, greased pig contests, sack races, foot races and fireworks, community and area leaders in the dusty Eastern Oregon town conceived the idea of an annual event to be known as the Pendleton Round-Up.

The group decided to stage the Round-Up some time around the middle of September to allow the grain farmers time to complete their harvest, and the livestock people an opportunity to make a late summer check-up.

The Pendleton Round-Up has continued its tradition as a let-loose cowboy party. If you want to see calf roping, barrel racing, Brahma bull riding, Native American ceremonial pageantry or first-rate country music concerts in Northeastern Oregon- then you can't miss the Round-Up.

Farmer's Market Chanterelle Fettuccine

Prep time: 30 minutes
Cook time: 30 minutes

Mushroom Sauce:

4	tablespoons extra virgin olive oil	1½	cups boiling water
2	large shallots, thinly sliced	3	tablespoons butter
3	cloves of garlic, minced	¼	cup hazelnuts, chopped
1	large red pepper, thinly sliced lengthwise	1	cup Chanterelle mushrooms, sliced
1	cup kale, chopped	1	tablespoon rosemary, chopped
3	ounces sun-dried tomatoes	1	cup heavy cream
			salt and pepper to taste

1. Sauté shallots and garlic in 3 tablespoons olive oil until translucent.
2. Add red pepper slices and kale and cook until tender. Set aside.
3. In a glass bowl, place sun-dried tomatoes in 1 ½ cups of boiling water for 5 minutes.
4. Squeeze water from tomatoes and chop. Reserve liquid.
5. Place butter and 1 tablespoon olive oil into the same pan and combine hazelnuts, Chanterelles, and rosemary. Add sun-dried tomatoes and cook until tender.
6. Add sun-dried tomato soaking liquid and cream and stir until thick. Add salt and pepper to taste.
7. Add shallots, garlic, red pepper and kale, heat to combine.

Pasta:

½   pound fettuccine
     Freshly grated Parmesan cheese to taste

1. Cook pasta in salted, boiling water until al dente.

Assembly:

1. Place pasta in large serving bowl, pour mushroom sauce on top. Gently toss with tongs.
2. Top with grated Parmesan cheese and serve immediately.

Yield: 4 servings

Rogue River Cedar Planked Salmon in Sweet and Sour Dill Sauce

Prep time: 10 minutes
Cook time: 15 minutes

Sweet and Sour Dill Sauce:

2   sprigs fresh dill, chopped
1   large clove of garlic, minced
3   tablespoons Dijon mustard
½   cup mayonnaise
¼   cup brown sugar
2   tablespoons capers
     juice of 1 lemon
     salt and pepper to taste

1.   Mix together: dill, garlic, mustard, mayonnaise, brown sugar, capers and lemon juice.

Salmon:

1   large salmon filet
1   grilling cedar plank
2   tablespoons olive oil

1.   Brush salmon filet with olive oil and season with salt and pepper.
2.   Place salmon on cedar plank and place on barbecue grill over medium heat.
3.   Baste salmon with sauce.
4.   Grill salmon until desired doneness. Approximately 15 minutes for medium.
5.   Serve with remaining sauce.

Yield: 4 servings

Mt. Angel Oktoberfest

A small community just southeast of Portland that German immigrants settled in the mid-19th century lets its hair down for four days in mid-September every year. Since 1965 the Mt. Angel Oktoberfest has celebrated the fall harvest with the same beer guzzling and entertainment that made it an Oregon tradition.

Mt. Angel is an adorable German-style village throughout the year, but during the festival 30 bands play on four stages and people dance in the streets between trips to the beer and wine "gartens." There is no food shortage here, as 60 vendors stand ready to feed the masses of partygoers. Oktoberfest also has rides for children, a classic car cruise-in and a German arts and crafts fair.

Apple Stuffed Pork Loin With Raspberry Sauce

Prep time: 15 minutes
Cook time: 1 hour 25 minutes
Oven: 325 degrees

Pork Loin:

1	cup onion, chopped	¼	teaspoon cardamom
2	stalks celery, chopped	4	cups dry bread cubes
½	cup butter	½	cup pecans
2	medium apples, chopped	1	3-4 lb. boneless pork loin roast
½	teaspoon allspice		garlic powder and salt & pepper to taste

1. For stuffing: in a large skillet cook onion and celery in butter until vegetables are tender, but not brown.
2. Stir in apples, allspice, and cardamom. Cook uncovered for approximately 5 minutes.
3. Transfer mixture into large bowl. Add bread cubes and pecans. Toss gently to coat and set aside.
4. Split roast lengthwise almost through; lay flat.
5. Spoon half of the stuffing over meat. Spoon the remaining half into a casserole dish.
6. Fold roast and tie with string. Place on rack and insert meat thermometer. Sprinkle with garlic powder, salt and pepper.
7. Roast uncovered in 325 degree oven until thermometer registers 160-170 degrees.
8. Put extra stuffing in oven the last 40 minutes.

Sauce:

2	cups fresh raspberries or un-drained frozen raspberries	2	tablespoons brandy
½	cup red currant jelly	1	tablespoon honey
½	cup apricot nectar	4	teaspoons cornstarch
		1	tablespoon water

1. For sauce: cook raspberries, red currant jelly, apricot nectar, brandy and honey over medium heat until mixture comes to a boil. Strain to remove seeds.
2. In separate bowl combine 4 teaspoons cornstarch and 1 tablespoon water. Stir into raspberry mixture.
3. Cook and stir until thickened and bubbly. Spoon over meat and serve.

Yield: 6-8 servings

Oven Roasted Halibut with Fennel, Tomatoes and Basil

Prep time: 10 minutes
Cook time: 25 minutes
Oven: 425 degrees

Halibut:
1½ pounds fresh halibut, skinned and cut into 2 inch cubes
1   tablespoon olive oil
1   garlic clove, minced
⅓   teaspoon dried red pepper, crushed (optional)
2   shallots, sliced
1   fennel bulb, coarsely chopped
1   14.5 ounce can diced tomatoes with balsamic vinegar, basil and olive oil
1   cup clam juice
20   Kalamata olives, pitted, quartered

1. Preheat oven to 425 degrees.
2. Sprinkle fish with salt and pepper.
3. Heat olive oil in heavy, oven proof skillet.
4. Add garlic and crushed red pepper and sauté for 2 minutes.
5. Add shallots and fennel. Sauté until shallots are tender, about 5 minutes.
6. Add canned tomatoes with juices and clam juice.
7. Simmer until fennel is tender and liquid reduces slightly.
8. Stir in olives.
9. Arrange halibut on top of tomato mixture.
10. Bake for 15 minutes or until the fish is opaque in center.
11. Make tomato and basil sauce.
12. Spoon tomato basil sauce over the top of fish and cook for an additional 2-3 minutes.
13. Serve immediately.

Tomato and Basil Sauce:
2   tablespoons fresh basil, chopped
2   medium, fresh tomatoes, chopped
2   tablespoons balsamic vinegar
1   tablespoon extra virgin olive oil
     salt and pepper to taste

1. Mix fresh basil, fresh tomatoes, balsamic vinegar and olive oil. Add salt and pepper to taste.

Yield: 4 servings

THE OREGON SHAKESPEARE FESTIVAL

Every year between late April and the waning days of October, the hip Southern Oregon town of Ashland bursts to life with live theatrical performances at the Oregon Shakespeare Festival. During the season, hundreds of company members produce eleven plays on three stages, ranging from Shakespearean classics like "Twelfth Night" to modern works like "Gibraltar" by Octavio Solis.

Time magazine ranked the OSF among the top five regional theatres in the U.S., and a Washington Post staff writer quipped, "This has got to be the only place in the world where whitewater rafting outfitters volunteer the information that they guarantee to have you back in time for Shakespeare."

Bard loyalists, some in period garb, pack the streets and hotels for this 70-year-old festival, which is the largest of its kind in the west. In addition to the plays, visitors can experience lectures, backstage tours and talks with the actors.

GEARHART STEAMED CLAMS WITH BACON AND BEER

Prep time: 5 minutes
Cook time: 15 minutes

CLAMS:

4	slices bacon
1	small yellow onion, chopped
3	pounds clams, scrubbed
½	bottle beer

1. Fry bacon in stock pot until soft and golden.
2. Add onion and continue cooking until bacon is nicely browned and onion is tender.
3. Stir in clams and add beer.
4. Cover and steam 6-7 minutes until the clams pop open.
5. Discard clams that do not open.
6. Stir gently to mix with bacon and onion.
7. Serve immediately.

Yield: 4 servings

Waterfront Smoked Salmon Quiche

Prep time: 20 minutes
Baking time: 45 minutes
Oven: 350 degrees

Crust:

1   9-inch pie crust shell

1.   Prepare crust according to directions on package.

Filling:

1   egg
4   teaspoons all purpose flour
½   cup mayonnaise
½   cup milk
1   cup Gruyere cheese, grated
1   cup smoked salmon, flaked
1½   tablespoons green onion, chopped
¼   teaspoon paprika

1.   Preheat oven to 350 degrees.
2.   Beat egg with a wire whisk.
3.   Blend in flour and mayonnaise.
4.   Add milk and blend well.
5.   Fold in cheese, smoked salmon and onion.
6.   Fill pie crust.
7.   Bake for 45 minutes or until toothpick inserted in center comes out clean.
8.   Sprinkle with paprika and serve.

Yield: 6 servings

PORTLAND CENTER STAGE

The Portland Center Stage is the city's leading professional theater company and is one of the largest regional theater companies in the nation. It is an affiliate of the League of Regional Theatres, Actor's Equity Association and Theatre Communications Group. Portland Center Stage produces a blend of classical, contemporary and premiere works in addition to its annual summer playwrights festival.

Golden Pumpkin Pancakes

Prep time: 10 minutes
Cook time: 10 minutes

Pancakes:

2   eggs
2   cups flour
4   teaspoons baking powder
1   teaspoon baking soda
1   teaspoon salt
1   tablespoon sugar
2   cups buttermilk
2   tablespoons vegetable oil
⅔   cup pureed pumpkin
1   teaspoon cinnamon
1   teaspoon ground cloves
1   teaspoon ground ginger
1   teaspoon ground nutmeg

1. Beat eggs with wire whisk.
2. Add to eggs: flour, baking powder, baking soda, salt, sugar, buttermilk, oil, pumpkin, cinnamon, cloves, ginger and nutmeg.
3. Heat griddle to 350 degrees.
4. Oil griddle with remaining oil as needed.
5. Ladle batter onto griddle.
6. Flip when edges stand up and top begins to bubble.
7. Serve with butter and warm maple syrup.
8. Freeze leftover batter in ⅔ cup portions for a quick breakfast on a weekday!

Yield: 20, 4 inch pancakes.

Pumpkin and White Chocolate Drops

Prep time: 15 minutes
Baking time: 14-18 minutes
Oven: 375 degrees

Drops:

2	cups sugar
2	cups butter, softened
2	cups pumpkin, pureed
2	eggs
4	cups flour
2	tablespoons pumpkin pie spice
1	teaspoon baking powder
½	teaspoon baking soda
1½	cups white chocolate chips
2	cups prepared cream cheese frosting
¼	cup brown sugar, packed

1. Preheat oven to 375 degrees.
2. Cream sugar and butter until light and fluffy.
3. Add pumpkin and eggs and mix until smooth.
4. Add flour, pumpkin spice, baking powder, and baking soda.
5. Mix well.
6. Stir in chocolate chips.
7. Drop rounded teaspoonfuls 2" apart on greased cookie sheet.
8. Bake 14-18 minutes.
9. Cool for 1 minute and remove from cookie sheet to wire rack.
10. Combine frosting and brown sugar in small bowl.
11. Spread a dollop on each warm cookie.

Yield: 6 dozen

ANTIQUING IN SELLWOOD

ANTIQUING IN SELLWOOD

Just a few miles up the Willamette River from downtown Portland is a warm, classic neighborhood called Sellwood. In the last few years Sellwood has burgeoned with popular restaurants and a strip of antique vendors (over two dozen) along Southeast 13th Avenue.

Collectors flock in droves to Sellwood to check out the variety of merchandise crowding every shop and window display. Shops feature everything from classic quilts to nautical items, and 1950s and 60s apparel to continental housewares. When you've grown weary of admiring old time treasures, have a freshly squeezed greyhound or a glass of wine at one of the many bistros in the area.

CHILLED APRICOT TORTE

Prep time: 20 minutes
Baking time: 35 minutes
Chill time: 1-4 hours

CRUST:
½   cup butter
½   cup sugar
1   egg
1   teaspoon vanilla
1½   cups flour

1.   Spray tart pan with removable bottom with non-stick cooking spray
2.   Cream softened butter, egg, sugar and vanilla.
3.   Add flour and mix to dough consistency.
4.   Press into tart pan.
5.   Bake for 10 minutes or until lightly browned.
6.   Cool.

FILLING:
1   15 ounce can apricots, drained
2   eggs
1   cup sour cream
½   cup sugar

1.   Arrange apricots cut side up on crust.
2.   Whisk eggs, sour cream and sugar until well combined.
3.   Pour over the apricots.
4.   Bake for 20 minutes to set.
5.   Broil until slightly browned on top.
6.   Chill before serving.

Yield: 8 servings

Umatilla Apple Cake

Prep time: 20 minutes
Baking time: 1 hour

Cake:

4	cups apples, chopped
1	cup sugar
½	cup vegetable oil
1	cup walnuts, chopped
2	eggs, beaten
2	teaspoons vanilla
2	cups flour
2	teaspoons baking soda
2	teaspoons cinnamon
1	teaspoon salt

1. Mix apples and sugar.
2. Add vegetable oil, walnuts, eggs and vanilla.
3. Mix well.
4. Combine flour, baking soda, cinnamon and salt, in a separate bowl.
5. Add dry ingredients to apple mixture.
6. Pour batter into a greased, 9 x 9 pan and bake at 350 degrees for 1 hour or until a toothpick inserted in center comes out clean.
7. Serve warm with whipped cream or caramel sauce.

Yield: 16 servings

Lighting Pioneer Square

Pear and Hazelnut Baked Brie

Lewis and Clark Herb Roasted Lamb *with Pinot Noir Sauce*

Dijon and Brown Sugar Glazed Carrots

Herbed Potato Soufflé

Pear Tart

Each year during the holiday season, Portlanders gather daily in "Portland's Living Room" at Pioneer Courthouse Square to celebrate the season and honor the cultural diversity in Portland. Portlanders take this time to celebrate with family and friends and to open their doors and hearts to new friends with scrumptious holiday dinners.

Festivities start on the Friday evening after Thanksgiving with the lighting of the Holiday Tree and continue throughout the season as celebrations for Hanukkah and Kwanzaa light up the square. Choirs sing, bands play and the Saturday Market relocates to Pioneer Square to offer shoppers a special opportunity to purchase one of a kind gifts! On December 31st, Portlanders ring in the New Year with a spectacular outdoor party with dancing and fireworks.

Pear and Hazelnut Baked Brie

Prep time: 15 minutes
Cook time: 20 minutes
Oven: 425 degrees

Brie:

1	18 ounce round Brie cheese	¼	cup and ¾ cup Oregon
2	frozen pie crust shells		Grower's & Shipper's Pear
1	fresh pear, sliced		and Hazelnut Fruit Spread*

1. Thaw the frozen pie crusts.
2. Bring Brie to room temperature.
3. Preheat oven to 425 degrees.
4. Cut a circle out of one of the pie crusts in the size of the Brie round.
5. Place the larger, uncut pie crust on an oiled baking sheet.
6. Spread ¼ cup fruit spread on uncut pie crust.
7. Place Brie on top of large crust and fruit spread.
8. Spread ¾ cup fruit spread on top of the Brie.
9. Place fresh pear slices on top of fruit spread and Brie.
10. Bring larger bottom pie crust up and around other ingredients.
11. Pinch edges of crust around on top so pie crust is sealed around other ingredients.
12. Use a cookie cutter to cut decorative shapes out of the pie crust circle in step 4.
13. Decorate top of pastry with the cutouts and brush with milk.
14. Bake at 425 degrees for 25 minutes or until pastry is golden brown and Brie is melted.
15. Let cool for 5 minutes and serve on platter. Brie may be sliced into wedges before serving.
16. Serve with pears, apples and toasted baguette slices.

*Other pear fruit spread or cranberry fruit spread work well with this recipe also.

Yield: 8-12 servings

Fireside Shrimp Dip

Prep time: 5 minutes
Chill: 1 hour

Dip:
1   3-ounce package softened cream cheese
1   cup sour cream
2   teaspoons lemon juice
1   package Italian salad dressing mix (dry)
1   cup frozen or fresh bay shrimp, rinsed

1.   Combine cream cheese, sour cream, lemon juice, dressing mix, and shrimp.
2.   Chill for 1 hour and serve with crackers or vegetables.

Yield: 12-15 servings

THE GROTTO'S CHRISTMAS FESTIVAL OF LIGHTS

The Grotto, a 62-acre national Catholic sanctuary in Northeast Portland, hosts over 60,000 visitors during the holiday season for its legendary Christmas celebration.

The festival features spectacular lights, hourly music concerts, outdoor caroling, a petting zoo and other family entertainment. The Grotto's pristine garden setting with magnificent architecture, towering firs, and an angel-covered cliff side burst with light during the holiday season.

SPINACH AND POMEGRANATE SALAD

Prep time: 20 minutes

DRESSING:

4	tablespoons cranberry juice concentrate, undiluted
4	tablespoons rice vinegar
1½	teaspoon Dijon mustard
1	teaspoon garlic, chopped
¼	teaspoon black pepper
½	cup canola oil
	salt to taste

1. Combine cranberry juice, rice vinegar, Dijon mustard, garlic, pepper, oil and salt in a jar or tightly sealed plastic container and shake.

SALAD:

8	cups baby spinach leaves
1	avocado, thinly sliced (optional)
½	cup red onion, thinly sliced
1	cup pomegranate seeds*
½	cup dried cranberries

1. Place spinach in a bowl, and top with pomegranate seeds.
2. Sprinkle cranberries and red onion on top.
3. Add avocado just before tossing.
4. Toss salad and add dressing to taste.

*To seed the pomegranate, slice through the outer skin as if to quarter. Then crack open into quarters with hands. Gently work seeds from casing with fingers while submerged in a bowl of water to keep from squirting self with the staining juice.

Yield: 6-8 servings

Toasted Hazelnut Sweet Potatoes

Prep time: 1 hour
Cook time: 1½ hours
Oven: 350 degrees

Potatoes:

4-5	sweet potatoes or yams (4 cups cooked)
½	cup white sugar
3	large eggs
2	teaspoons vanilla
8	tablespoons butter plus 2 tablespoons butter
¼	cup flour
½	cup hazelnuts, chopped
½	cup sweetened flake coconut
½	cup brown sugar

1. Boil the sweet potatoes or yams until soft.
2. Peel and place in mixing bowl with sugar, eggs, vanilla and butter.
3. Mix on low speed for two minutes until the mixture is smooth.
4. Place in 1-quart casserole dish.
5. Mix remaining 2 tablespoons butter, flour, nuts, coconut and brown sugar in a 1-quart pot over low heat.
6. If needed add more flour to make the topping crumbly.
7. Add to top of sweet potatoes or yams and cook at 350 degrees for 45-60 minutes.
8. Can be refrigerated for up to one day before cooking.

Yield: 8 servings

PORTLAND'S PITTOCK MANSION

In 1853, an Englishman named Henry Lewis Pittock crossed the great western wilderness by wagon train from Pennsylvania to Oregon. Pittock settled in Portland as a penniless 19-year-old and later came to own the Weekly Oregonian, which is now the Oregonian, and dabbled in other industries including railroads, real estate and banking.

Pittock and his wife, Georgiana, amassed a fortune through their ventures and built a monolithic, 46-acre residence high in the wooded hills above Portland. The mansion itself was completed in 1914 and was built mainly by Oregon craftsmen and artisans who utilized Northwest materials to build the house. A visit to the Pittock Mansion offers visitors fabulous views of Portland and the Cascade Mountains. In addition to a chance to tour the residence which still stands as a turn-of-the-century architectural marvel, The Pittock Mansion Society encourages visitors to bring a picnic lunch and bask in the sun on the perfectly polished mansion grounds or take a hike on the surrounding wilderness trails.

HERBED POTATO SOUFFLÉ

Prep time: 30 minutes
Cook time: 45 minutes
Oven: 350 degrees

SOUFFLÉ:

6   large Russet potatoes
½   cup butter (1 stick)
¾   pound cheddar cheese, grated
2   cups sour cream
1   bunch green onions, chopped including much of the greens
2   tablespoons fresh rosemary, minced
2   tablespoons fresh thyme, minced
1   tablespoon salt
¾   teaspoon white pepper
2   tablespoons butter

1.   Boil potatoes in skins until barely done (do not over cook).
2.   Let potatoes cool.
3.   Peel and grate potatoes.
4.   In a microwave, melt butter and cheese.
5.   In a large bowl, combine butter and cheese mixture with the sour cream, onions, 1 tablespoon of the rosemary and 1 tablespoon of the thyme. Add salt and pepper.
6.   Mix in potatoes.
7.   Spoon into a greased 3-quart casserole dish.
8.   Dot top with remaining butter.
9.   Baked uncovered at 350 degrees for 45 minutes.
10. Sprinkle with remaining rosemary and thyme and serve.

Yield: 6-8 servings

Dijon and Brown Sugar Glazed Carrots

Prep time: 15 minutes
Cook time: 20-30 minutes

Carrots:

6   carrots

1. Peel and diagonally cut carrots.
2. Steam until just tender, about 15 minutes.

Brown Sugar Glaze:

2   tablespoons butter
¼   cup brown sugar
2   tablespoons Dijon mustard
¼   teaspoon salt
2   teaspoons fresh parsley, minced

1. Melt butter in a large skillet, stir in brown sugar, mustard and salt.
2. Stir in carrots.
3. Heat over medium-low heat, stirring constantly until thoroughly heated and nicely glazed, about 5-8 minutes.
4. Sprinkle with fresh chopped parsley and serve.

Yield: 4-6 servings

Roasted Acorn Squash with Harvest Apples and Currants

Prep time: 20 minutes
Cook time: 50 minutes
Oven: 400 degrees

Squash:
2   acorn squash
       boiling water

1.   Preheat oven to 400 degrees.
2.   Wash squash and halve lengthwise.
3.   Scoop out seeds and fibers.
4.   Put squash halves into baking dish, cut side down, and add about ½ inch of boiling water to the dish.
5.   Bake at 400 degrees for 20 minutes.

Stuffing:
3   tart apples
1   cup currants
1   tablespoon cinnamon
1   teaspoon ground nutmeg
½   cup melted butter plus 1-2 tablespoons
½   cup honey
       salt to taste

1.   While squash is baking, prepare stuffing. Peel, core and dice apples.
2.   Mix apples and currants with cinnamon, nutmeg, and ¼ cup melted butter and honey.
3.   Turn acorn squash halves cut side up in baking dish and brush with remaining melted butter then sprinkle with salt. Fill each acorn squash half with apple and honey mixture. (Leave water in bottom of baking dish)
4.   Cover baking dish with aluminum foil and continue baking at 400 degrees for 30 minutes longer, until squash and apples are tender.

Yield: 4 servings

Herbed-Crusted Pork Medallions with Mustard Sauce

Prep time: 20 minutes
Cook time: 20 minutes

Breaded Pork:

8   (3 ounce) boneless center cut pork medallions or chops
1   cup herbed bread crumbs
2   tablespoons fresh rosemary, chopped
2   tablespoons fresh parsley, chopped
2   tablespoons fresh thyme, chopped
½   tablespoon fresh oregano, chopped
4   teaspoons garlic powder
2   teaspoons salt
1   teaspoon pepper
½   cup melted butter
     olive oil

1. Place bread crumbs in a food processor and pulse to a fine blend.
2. Add rosemary, parsley, thyme, oregano, garlic powder, salt and pepper.
3. Pulse 30 seconds and set aside.
4. Heat olive oil in a 10" skillet.
5. Dip each medallion in butter then crumb mixture and sauté 5 minutes on each side.

Mustard Sauce:

1½ cups heavy cream
4   tablespoons Dijon mustard

1. Pour cream into a sauté pan.
2. Add mustard and reduce by ⅓.
3. Continue cooking over medium heat for 2-3 minutes more, stirring constantly.
4. Arrange medallions on plate and drizzle with sauce.

Yield: 4-6 servings

The Portland Christmas Ships

During the holidays, Portlanders know you can head for the waterfront for the annual parade of Christmas ships. For over 50 years local skippers have been outfitting their boats in Christmas lights and parading up and down the Columbia and Willamette Rivers for two weeks in December.

Restaurants along the parade routes see huge crowds each night for the 50-60 vessel event. Many large Portland area corporations plan their annual company holiday parties to coincide with the Christmas Ship schedule, while private residents also hold nightly parties to view the ships on both rivers.

If you're apt to throw on a jacket and grab a cup of hot cocoa, you can sit on the riverbanks and enjoy one of the largest and longest-running floating holiday shows in the nation.

Spinach and Sun-Dried Tomato Stuffed Beef Tenderloin with Sherry Sauce

Prep time: 15 minutes
Oven: 425 degrees
Cook time: 1 to 1½ hours

Beef Tenderloin and Stuffing:

1	yellow onion, chopped
2	tablespoons vegetable oil
½	pound fresh spinach
½	teaspoon salt
½	teaspoon pepper
¼	cup Parmesan cheese, grated
¼	cup chopped oil-packed sun-dried tomatoes, drained
1	3-4 pound of beef tenderloin

1. Preheat oven to 425 degrees.
2. In a large skillet, cook onion in vegetable oil until tender.
3. Add spinach, salt and pepper. Cook until spinach wilts.
4. Remove from heat and stir in Parmesan cheese and sun-dried tomatoes.
5. Make lengthwise cut in center of tenderloin, cutting almost in half, but not all the way through. Lay open, spread with spinach mixture, and fold to enclose filling. Tie with string.
6. Place cut side up in roasting pan. Cover stuffing with foil to prevent drying out.
7. Cook 1 hour to 1 ½ hours, or until meat thermometer registers desired degree of doneness.
8. Remove from oven and let sit 15 minutes. Roast will continue cooking so remove from oven, one doneness down from your desired doneness.
9. Slice meat and place on serving platter. Drizzle sauce over roast.

SAUCE:

1   cup beef broth
¼   cup dry sherry

1. To make sauce, skim fat from pan drippings and add beef broth and sherry.
2. Heat to boiling, stirring to loosen brown bits, reduce to 1 cup.
3. Strain sauce through fine mesh sieve.
4. Return to heat until hot.

Note: The stuffing can be prepared a couple of days ahead and stuffed into the roast before cooking.

Yield: 4-6 servings

Lewis and Clark Herb Roasted Lamb with Pinot Noir Sauce

Prep time: 20 minutes
Cook time: 1 hr. 15 mins. *or until meat thermometer is at your preferred doneness*
Oven: 400 degrees

Lamb:

1   leg of domestic lamb with bone (3-4 pounds)
¼   cup fresh lemon juice
7   cloves of garlic, minced
4   tablespoons rosemary leaves, chopped
1   tablespoon salt
2   teaspoons black pepper, coarsely ground

1. Preheat oven to 400 degrees.
2. Using your hands, rub the lamb all over with the lemon juice.
3. Pat the garlic and rosemary evenly all over the surface of the meat.
4. Season the lamb with salt and pepper and place the lamb in a roasting pan.
5. Roast the lamb for 30 minutes.
6. Reduce oven temperature to 350 degrees and continue to cook for 30-40 minutes until meat thermometer registers 140 degrees (rare). (Do not let the thermometer touch the bone).
7. Remove the lamb and let rest for 15 minutes, which will allow the lamb to continue cooking to medium rare.

Sauce:

1	cup green onions, diced
½	cup fresh thyme, chopped
½	cup pinot noir
½	cup fresh rosemary, chopped
1	cup chicken stock

1. While lamb is resting, place roasting pan over stove burners.
2. Add onion to pan and stir to combine with pan drippings. Sauté until onions are tender.
3. Add chicken stock and wine to deglaze the pan, scraping the bottom of the pan with a wooden spoon to release any particles.
4. Reduce the mixture over high heat until the sauce thickens slightly.
5. Add chopped rosemary and thyme and heat sauce to a boil. Remove from heat.
6. Strain before serving.
7. Carve meat and serve with the sauce drizzled over lamb.

Yield: 8 to 12 servings

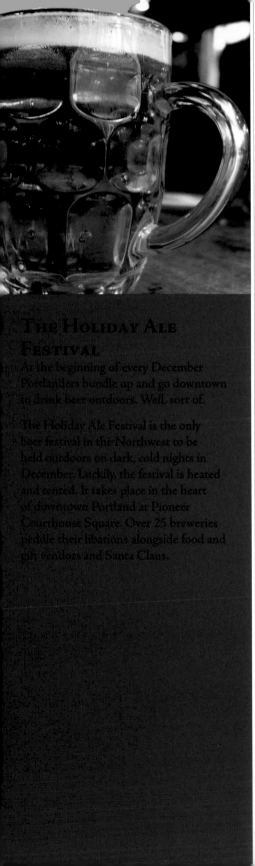

THE HOLIDAY ALE
FESTIVAL

At the beginning of every December
Portlanders bundle up and go downtown
to drink beer outdoors. Well, sort of.

The Holiday Ale Festival is the only
beer festival in the Northwest to be
held outdoors on dark, cold nights in
December. Luckily, the festival is heated
and tented. It takes place in the heart
of downtown Portland at Pioneer
Courthouse Square. Over 25 breweries
peddle their libations alongside food and
gift vendors and Santa Claus.

CURRIED PACIFIC SEAFOOD
EN CROUTE

Prep time: 15 minutes
Cook time: 35 minutes
Oven: 425 degrees

SEAFOOD EN CROUTE:

8 ounces halibut	2 ounces fresh bay shrimp, cooked and rinsed
4 ounces smoked salmon	
1 cup coconut milk	½ cup peas
2 cups skim milk	1 tablespoon butter
2 shallots	1 tablespoon flour
4 ounces mushrooms	½ teaspoon yellow curry paste
1 tablespoon butter	salt and pepper to taste
	frozen puff pastry dough (defrosted)

1. Preheat oven to 425 degrees.
2. Put halibut, salmon, coconut milk, and skim milk in a large saucepan.
3. Bring to a boil. Simmer 5 to 10 minutes, until fish flakes.
4. Chop shallots and slice mushrooms.
5. Sauté shallots in 1 tablespoon butter until soft, about 2 minutes.
6. Add mushrooms and continue sautéing for 3 minutes.
7. Reserve 1 cup of the fish liquid.
8. Drain fish and flake, removing skin and bones.
9. Add shrimp, sautéed shallots, mushrooms and peas to flaked fish.
10. Melt 1 tablespoon butter.
11. Add 1 tablespoon flour. Cook gently for 1 minute.
12. Add 1 cup reserved fish liquid.
13. Return to boil stirring continuously until thickened, 2-3 minutes.
14. Add ½ teaspoon yellow curry paste.
15. Add salt and pepper to taste.
16. Combine fish mixture with sauce.
17. Put in pie pan and top with puff pastry. Brush top with milk.
18. Bake at 425 degrees for 35 minutes, until top is golden brown.

Yield: 4-6 servings

Bandon-by-the-Sea Cranberry and White Chocolate Scones

Prep time: 45 minutes
Cook time: 20-30 minutes
Oven: 350 degrees

Scones:

6   cups all purpose flour
1   cup granulated sugar
2   tablespoons baking powder
1½   teaspoons salt
¾   cup chilled unsalted butter (1½ sticks)
1⅓   cups dried cranberries
1¼   cups white chocolate chips
1¾   cups whipping cream
3   eggs
1   tablespoon vanilla

1. Preheat oven to 350 degrees.
2. Sift together flour, sugar, baking powder and salt.
3. Cut in butter with pastry blender until consistency of dry oatmeal.
4. Add dried cranberries and white chocolate chips, mix lightly with a fork.
5. In a medium bowl combine cream, eggs and vanilla.
6. Add dry ingredients. Stir until dough just comes together (if dry add slightly more cream, 1 tablespoon at a time).
7. On a board, knead gently 5-6 times. Do not overwork.
8. Divide into desired size pans. This amount works out to fill 3 9-inch pans, cut into 8 wedges and pulled slightly apart.
9. Bake 20-30 minutes or until toothpick comes out clean.

Yield: 24 servings

Peacock Lane

If you aren't ready to commit every December to Portland's most famous neighborhood lights display, then don't move to Northeast Portland's Peacock Lane. Since 1929, onlookers have driven or walked by all 31 homes on Peacock Lane that are illuminated for the holidays. Each neighbor conjures his or her own unique design and theme.

Black Cherry Tea Truffles with Hazelnuts

Prep time: 20 minutes
Chill time: 2 hours

Truffles:

⅔   cup heavy cream
2   tablespoons unsalted butter, cut into 4 pieces and softened
2   teaspoons loose black cherry tea leaves
6   ounces fine quality (imported) bittersweet chocolate (not unsweetened)
1   cup dried cherries, chopped fine
1   cup hazelnuts - ground in coffee grinder or food processor until finely ground

1. Bring cream and butter to a boil in a small heavy saucepan and stir in tea leaves.
2. Remove from heat and let steep for 5 minutes.
3. Meanwhile, finely grind chocolate in food processor and transfer to a bowl.
4. Pour cream through a fine-mesh sieve onto chocolate, pressing on and discarding tea leaves, then whisk until smooth.
5. Add chopped cherries.
6. Cover ganache and chill until firm, about 2 hours.
7. Spoon level teaspoons of ganache onto a baking sheet.
8. Put hazelnuts into a bowl.
9. Drop ganache by teaspoon into the nuts and roll into a ball. Transfer coated balls into an airtight container, separating layers with waxed paper.

* Loose tea leaves tend to be of higher quality than tea bags, giving the truffles a fresher, more distinct flavor.
Can be chilled in refrigerator for about a week.
Can be frozen for up to a month.

Yield: 2-3 dozen

Tiramisu Delicioso e Semplice

Prep time: 30 minutes
Chill time: 1 hour up to 1 day

Syrup:
6   tablespoons coffee liqueur
3   tablespoons sugar
1   tablespoon water
2   teaspoons instant coffee or espresso powder

1.   Combine liqueur, sugar, water, and coffee in a small bowl and stir together until the instant coffee dissolves.

Filling:
2   8-ounce packages cream cheese
1   cup sugar plus 1 tablespoon

1.   Combine cream cheese, sugar and whisk to blend.

Cake:
5   half-inch slices pound cake (can be purchased)
2   teaspoons chocolate shavings

1.   Place pieces of cake on the bottom of a 9 x 9 square cake pan, spoon some of the syrup mixture over the cake to soak in. Spread ⅓ of filling over cake. Place another layer of cake, soak with syrup mixture and top with the next ⅓ filling, then put on another layer, finishing with the last filling on top.*
2.   Sprinkle chocolate shavings over the top.
3.   Serve immediately or cover and refrigerate up to one day.

*Note: depending on the width of the cake pan, 3 layers may or may not work.
It does not matter how many layers there are, and how much of the filling you use
in-between layers, just that the layering should happen in that order: cake, soak with
syrup, filling on top.

Yield: 8-12 servings

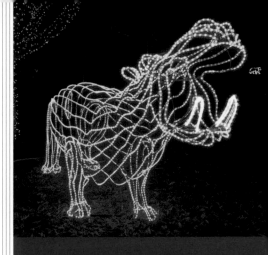

The Oregon Zoo's Zoolights Festival

Kids growing up in Portland have all taken at least one trip to Zoolights. Zoolights features a ride on the Oregon Zoo's brightly lit train through the zoo where families ogle at the holiday light displays all over the zoo property. In addition to the signature train ride, the zoo hosts hundreds of musical groups, costumed animal characters, an artist market, and seasonal goodies.

First Night Chocolate Torte

Prep time: 30 minutes
Cook time: 10 minutes
Oven: 350 degrees
Chill time: 2 hours

Crust:
2   cups crushed chocolate wafer cookies
½   cup butter, melted

1. Preheat oven to 350 degrees.
2. For crust, mix two cups of crushed chocolate wafer cookies and melted butter. Pour over bottom of 8-inch spring form pan and bake at 350 degrees for 10 minutes.

Filling:
6   ounces semisweet chocolate
2   ounces unsweetened chocolate
6   tablespoons water
6   eggs, separated
2   teaspoons grated orange peel
4   tablespoons orange flavored liqueur
½   teaspoon cream of tartar
½   cup sugar

1. Put chocolate squares and 6 tablespoons water in a double boiler. Set over hot (not boiling) water, stirring occasionally until chocolate melts.
2. Slightly beat egg yolks and add to chocolate, blending in smoothly with a wire whisk.
3. Remove from heat and stir in orange peel and liqueur. Set aside.
4. Beat egg whites and cream of tartar until foamy. Gradually add sugar and beat until egg whites hold soft peaks.
5. Stir ⅓ of the egg whites into the chocolate and gently fold in the remaining egg whites.
6. Pour chocolate mixture into crust and freeze for a minimum of 2 hours. Remove from freezer 15 minutes before serving.

Yield: 6-8 servings

Pear Tart

Prep time: 45 minutes
Cook time: 35 minutes
Oven: 350 and 375 degrees

Crust:

½ cup butter, softened
⅓ cup sugar
¼ teaspoon vanilla
¾ cup flour
⅔ cup pecans, finely chopped
   cooking spray

1. Preheat oven to 350 degrees.
2. Cream butter and sugar together.
3. Spray tart pan with cooking spray.
4. Add vanilla, flour and pecans and press into a 9-inch tart pan.
5. Pierce all over with a fork.
6. Bake crust for 10 minutes at 350 degrees. Cool slightly.
7. Increase oven to 375 degrees.

Filling:

8 ounces cream cheese, softened
1 egg
1½ teaspoons vanilla
2 tablespoons sugar
1 pound pear halves
2 teaspoons sugar mixed with 1 teaspoon cinnamon

1. Beat cream cheese and eggs slightly.
2. Add vanilla and sugar.
3. Spread over crust.
4. Slice pears thinly and arrange in a pinwheel design on top of filling.
5. Sprinkle with sugar and cinnamon mixture.
6. Bake at 375 degrees for 25 minutes.
7. Cool and refrigerate.

Yield: 8 servings

There's no Place like Home

First Thursday in the Pearl

Sun-Dried Tomato Pesto *with Toast Points*

Hazelnut and Gorgonzola Salad

Crab and Chanterelle Chowder

Duniway Chocolate Cake

Northwest Portland's Soho-like warehouse district, the Pearl, gets trampled with artists and onlookers on the first Thursday of every month, rain or shine. Galleries in the Pearl put sculpture, painting, photography, etchings and drawings on view and stay open into the evening hours. Fabulous local restaurants and retailers follow suit and remain open hoping to entice the chic art lovers. Many galleries also provide complimentary drinks and small bites.

Urban legend has it that the name, The Pearl, came when a local developer used the phrase to describe the beautiful artists' lofts that were lodged in the aging warehouses, like a pearl in a shell! Portlanders get together with their friends to see and be seen in the galleries. They then gather in spectacular lofts and condominiums for a casual meal to extol Portland's hot art scene.

Rosemary and Garlic Knots

Prep Time: 20 minutes
Cook Time: 17 minutes
Oven: 350 degrees

Garlic Knots

3   tablespoons butter
2   garlic cloves, minced
½   teaspoon garlic powder
1   (11 once) can refrigerated French bread dough
2   tablespoons fresh rosemary, chopped
2   tablespoons Parmesan cheese, grated
       cooking spray

1. Preheat oven to 350 degrees.
2. Melt butter in a small skillet over medium heat.
3. Add minced garlic; sauté 30 seconds or until lightly browned.
4. Remove from heat; stir in garlic powder.
5. Unroll the French bread dough onto a lightly floured surface; brush dough with garlic mixture.
6. Sprinkle the dough with rosemary and cheese.
7. Cut the dough crosswise into 12 strips.
8. Shape each strip into a knot.
9. Place the knots onto a baking sheet coated with cooking spray.
10. Bake for 17 minutes or until lightly browned. Serve warm.

You can make these rolls a day ahead, wrap them in foil, and reheat them in the oven at 350 degrees for 10 minutes.

Yield: 12 servings (serving size: 1 roll)

Sun-Dried Tomato Pesto

Prep Time: 20 minutes

Pesto:
4   ounces sun-dried tomatoes
2   tablespoons fresh basil, chopped
2   tablespoons fresh parsley, chopped
1   tablespoon garlic, chopped
¼   cup pine nuts
3   tablespoons onion, chopped
¼   cup balsamic vinegar
1   tablespoon tomato paste
⅓   cup tomatoes, crushed
¼   cup red wine
½   cup olive oil
½   cup grated Parmesan cheese

1.   In a food processor, combine sun-dried tomatoes, basil, parsley, garlic, pine nuts
     and onion.
2.   Process until well blended.
3.   Add vinegar, tomato paste, crushed tomatoes, red wine, and process.
4.   Add olive oil and Parmesan cheese and process.

Serving suggestion: Serve with toast points, crackers or over hot pasta.

Yield: 10-12 servings

CRAB AND CHANTERELLE CHOWDER

Prep Time: 15 minutes
Cook Time: 20 minutes

CHOWDER:

¾	pound Yukon gold potatoes, cubed into ¾ inch pieces
2	tablespoons olive oil
2	medium shallots, diced (about ½ cup)
¾	pound Chanterelle mushrooms, very roughly chopped (about 4 cups)
4	ounces tasso, or pancetta, diced
	salt and pepper to taste
6	cups clam juice
16	ounces of lump crab meat

1. Cover potatoes with lightly salted water and boil until tender. Drain potato water.
2. Set potatoes aside. In a large pot, heat oil over medium high heat.
3. Sauté shallots until translucent.
4. Add mushrooms, plus a dash of salt and pepper and sauté. The mushrooms will quickly absorb the oil but then begin to release their own juices.
5. Add the tasso or pancetta and continue to sauté.
6. Add clam juice.
7. Add the potatoes, mashing a handful of them to thicken the soup.
8. Add the crabmeat, and simmer on low for 15 minutes to bring flavors together.

Yield: 6-8 Servings

Hazelnut and Gorgonzola Salad

Prep Time: 15 minutes

Salad:
1   head romaine lettuce- torn into bite size pieces
2   red delicious apples, cubed
5   ounces gorgonzola cheese, crumbled
½   cup hazelnuts, coarsely chopped

1.   Combine lettuce, apples, cheese, and hazelnuts in a large bowl.

Dressing:
2   teaspoons Dijon mustard
2-3   garlic cloves, minced
¼   cup white wine vinegar
¼   teaspoon salt
¼   teaspoon pepper
⅓   cup olive oil

1.   Whisk together mustard, garlic, vinegar, salt, pepper and olive oil in a bowl and
      add to salad.
2.   Toss and serve chilled.

Yield: 4-6 people

The Japanese Garden

The Japanese Garden is tucked into Portland's West Hills. It is a haven of tranquil beauty that has been proclaimed one of the most authentic Japanese gardens outside of Japan. It has its own personality reflected in five formal garden styles set on five and one-half acres: the Strolling Pond Garden, the Natural Garden, the Sand and Stone Garden, the Flat Garden and the Tea Garden.

Designed in 1963 by Professor Takuma Tono, an internationally renowned authority on Japanese garden landscaping. The Garden opened to the public in 1967 as a place of serene, quiet beauty.

COLUMBIA RIVER GORGE NATIONAL SCENIC AREA

Anytime of year is the perfect time to take a short drive due east from Portland into the Columbia River Gorge. Put simply, this area is naturally striking.

The Columbia River Gorge is a monumental river canyon cutting the only sea-level route through the Cascade Mountains. It's 80 miles long and up to 4,000 feet deep with the north canyon walls in Washington and the south canyon walls in Oregon. This area is easily accessible to visitors and features hiking, mountain biking, windsurfing, camping, fishing, boating, wildlife watching, birding, wildflower viewing, photography, picnicking and rock climbing.

Be sure to also catch Multnomah Falls just off of I-84, which is the second highest year-round waterfall in the United States. Falls visitors can hike right up to the top of the falls and peek over the edge.

NOB HILL POTATOES

Prep Time: 20 minutes
Cook Time: 1 hour
Oven: 350 degrees

POTATOES:

5   cups diced cooked Russet potatoes
2   cups ricotta cheese
1   cup sour cream
⅓   cup green onions, sliced
1   small clove garlic, minced
2   tablespoons fresh thyme, chopped
2   teaspoons salt
½   cup shredded cheddar cheese
      Paprika to taste

1. Peel, dice and boil potatoes until soft.
2. Combine ricotta cheese, sour cream, green onions, garlic, thyme and salt.
3. Fold in potatoes.
4. Pour into a greased, flat 1 ½ quart casserole dish.
5. Top with cheese. Sprinkle Paprika over top.
6. Tent with foil; bake at 350 degrees for 40 minutes.

Yield: 10-12 servings

Coconut Rice with Ginger and Chiles

Prep Time: 15 minutes
Cook Time: 60 minutes

Rice:

¾ cup sweetened, shredded coconut
1 cup onion, finely chopped
1 teaspoon jalapeño pepper, ribbed, seeded and finely chopped
2 teaspoons fresh ginger, minced
1 tablespoon olive oil
2 cups long-grain rice, preferably basmati
1 teaspoon light rum (optional)
2 teaspoons salt
3½ cups unsweetened coconut milk mixed with 1 cup water (4 ½ cups total)
3 tablespoons fresh lime juice

1. Spread coconut in small skillet and toast over low heat stirring frequently until golden brown (about 5 minutes) Set aside to cool.
2. In heavy saucepan, sauté onions, jalapeño, and ginger in the oil over medium heat, stirring frequently, until onions are soft and translucent. About 5 minutes.
3. Add rice and cook, stirring 2 minutes more. Add rum and boil for about 5 seconds to burn off alcohol.
4. Stir in salt and 3 ½ cups of diluted coconut milk; bring to a boil.
5. Cover and reduce heat to lowest possible setting. Simmer for 20 minutes.
6. Add remaining diluted coconut milk and lime juice. Cover and cook 20 minutes until rice is tender.
7. Serve immediately, garnished with toasted coconut.

Can be prepared in advance and reheated.

Yield: 4 servings

Sour Cream Lemon Mushrooms

Prep Time: 10 minutes
Cook Time: 35 minutes
Oven: 350 degrees

Mushrooms:

½	cup butter
2	pounds sliced fresh button mushrooms
6	green onions, chopped
1	cup sour cream
2	tablespoons parsley, chopped
½	teaspoon salt
1	teaspoon lemon pepper
3	slices bread, toasted and crumbled
2	tablespoons melted butter

1. Preheat oven to 350 degrees.
2. Sauté mushrooms and onions in butter (about 3 minutes) add flour and stir.
3. Add sour cream, parsley, salt, lemon pepper and place in a casserole dish.
4. Sprinkle with crumbled bread and drizzle with 2 tablespoons melted butter.
5. Bake uncovered for 30 minutes.

Yield: 4-6 servings

Blue Lake Green Beans and Red Peppers with Balsamic Glaze

Prep Time: 15 minutes
Cook Time: 20 minutes

Beans:

1½   pounds green beans, rinsed and ends trimmed

1.   Steam beans over medium-high heat until partially cooked 4-5 minutes.
2.   Drain and immerse in ice-water to stop cooking.

Balsamic Glaze:

1   tablespoon olive oil
1   medium red pepper, cored, seeded and cut into strips
2   cloves garlic, minced
½   cup sherry
¼   cup balsamic vinegar
½   cup Parmesan cheese, grated
        salt and pepper

1.   In a sauté pan, add olive oil, red peppers and garlic. Sauté until tender.
2.   Add: sherry, balsamic vinegar, salt and pepper.
3.   Reduce heat and simmer until reduced to ¼ cup glaze.
4.   Add beans and sauté until beans are well coated and warmed through.
5.   Using a slotted spoon, transfer glazed beans and peppers to serving platter.
6.   Top with Parmesan cheese.

Yield: 4-6 servings

Tomato Curry Lamb on Egg Noodles

Prep Time: 10 minutes
Cook Time: 1½ hours

Lamb:

2   pounds domestic lamb cut into 1 inch pieces
2   tablespoons vegetable oil
2   cups tomato sauce
1   medium yellow onion, chopped
1   cup water
¾   teaspoon curry powder
1½   teaspoons salt
¼   teaspoon pepper
2   cups petit peas
1   package egg noodles
1   cup parsley, chopped

1.   Brown lamb in vegetable oil. Pour off drippings.
2.   Add tomato sauce, onion, water, curry powder, salt and pepper.
3.   Cover tightly and simmer for one hour.
4.   Add peas and simmer 20 minutes.
5.   Cook egg noodles according to directions on package.
6.   Spoon lamb curry over egg noodles and sprinkle with chopped parsley.
7.   Serve immediately.

Yield: 4-6 servings

Crab Cakes with Red Pepper Cream Sauce

Prep Time: 20 minutes
Cook Time: 25 minutes

Crab Cakes:

1   cup seasoned bread crumbs
2   large eggs lightly beaten
1½   cups crab meat
½   cup cilantro, finely chopped
4   scallions, chopped
¾   of a red pepper, seeded and diced
1   jalapeño pepper, seeded and diced (or use about 7 shakes of hot sauce)
⅔   cup mayonnaise
     salt and pepper to season

1. Combine bread crumbs, eggs, crab, cilantro, scallions, red pepper, jalapeño pepper, mayonnaise and season with salt and pepper to taste.
2. Form balls about the size of a golf ball and flatten slightly.
3. Place on cookie sheet that is lightly greased.
4. Bake for 15 minutes at 350 degrees.
5. Place on serving platter or individual plates.

Cream Sauce:

1   cup half and half
4   tablespoons butter
1   teaspoon dry sherry
1   teaspoon thyme
¼   teaspoon tarragon
3   pinches of salt
6-8 shakes of pepper
⅛   teaspoon garlic powder
½   of a red pepper, finely chopped
1½   teaspoon lemon juice
1   teaspoon Wondra flour to thicken

1. Combine half and half, butter, sherry, thyme, tarragon, salt, pepper, garlic powder, red pepper, and lemon juice and cook over medium heat for about 10 minutes.
2. Add Wondra flour, about 1 teaspoon, and simmer for another 5 minutes until creamy.
3. You can either serve the sauce separately or spoon on a plate and lay crab cakes on top. Serve hot.

Yield: 6 servings

Haystack Rock on the Oregon Coast

This towering monolith is one of the tallest in the world, second only to the Rock of Gibraltar in Spain. And yes, it does look like a big black haystack.

Standing at 235 feet and sitting right on the North Coast's Cannon Beach, this spectacle is the product of one of the Earth's largest lava flows. Haystack Rock is unmistakable as it sits almost awkwardly in the middle of the beach.

Haystack Rock is also a protected marine garden for tide pool dwellers and birds, so tourists are asked to tread lightly around barnacled rock. The rock does not stand alone, however, as neighboring rock formations, the Needles, rest nearby.

Astoria Ginger Prawns

Prep Time: 25 minutes
Marinate: 15 minutes
Broil: 6-7 minutes

Prawns:
1¾   pounds fresh prawns

Marinade:
3   tablespoons fresh lime juice
2   tablespoons teriyaki sauce
2   cloves garlic, crushed
2   teaspoons grated fresh ginger
2   teaspoons Asian sesame oil
   hot chile oil to taste

1. Place prawns in a non-metallic bowl. In a separate bowl, combine lime juice, teriyaki sauce, garlic, ginger, sesame oil and hot chile oil and whisk together well.
2. Pour over prawns, toss to coat evenly and cover bowl with plastic wrap.
3. Let stand at room temperature for 15 minutes.
4. Preheat broiler. Transfer prawns to broiler pan.
5. Spoon marinade on top of prawns and broil about 4 inches from heat for 6-7 minutes.
6. Serve immediately.

Yield: 4 as an entree

CHINESE GATE PORK WRAPS

Prep Time: 20 minutes
Marinate: 30 minutes or overnight
Cook Time: 15 minutes
Oven: 400 degrees

PORK:
8   ounces pork fillet
8   green onions

1. Gently pound meat to flatten
2. Cut pork into 20 thin slices
3. Trim green onion and cut into lengths the same size as pork
4. Roll each slice of pork. (Tie one strip of onion around each rolled slice of pork.)

SAUCE:
1   clove garlic, crushed
1   tablespoon soy sauce
1   tablespoon honey
1   tablespoon hoisin sauce
1   inch ginger, finely chopped

1. Mix garlic, soy sauce, honey, hoisin sauce and ginger in a shallow ovenproof dish.
2. Add pork wraps and marinate for at least 30 minutes (can marinate overnight in the fridge if you have the time).
3. Cook at 400 degrees for 10-15 minutes, basting as it cooks with the sauce in the pan.
4. Can serve warm or cold. (Great, served cold!)

Yield: 8 servings

CLASSICAL CHINESE GARDEN

Created to nurture and inspire all who visit, this Garden is little changed from what might have greeted you during the Ming dynasty in China. Portland's is an authentic Suzhou-style garden. It grew out of a friendship between Portland and Suzhou, a city renowned for its exquisite gardens.

This walled Garden encloses a full city block. Serpentine walkways, a bridged lake, and open colonnades set off meticulously arranged landscape of plants, water, stone, poetry, and buildings. Architects and artisans from China who designed and constructed the Garden mean for each aspect of the Garden to convey artistic effect and symbolic importance.

The design embodies the duality of nature, yin and yang. When these are balanced, harmony results. The yin and yang of the Garden take you to another place and time.

Spicy Asian Steamed Mussels

Prep Time: 15 minutes
Cook Time: 10 minutes

Mussels

5   pounds mussels
3   limes (⅓ cup juice)
1   3½ ounce can unsweetened coconut milk
½   cup dry white wine
1½   tablespoons Thai red curry paste
3   cloves of garlic, crushed
1   tablespoon fish sauce (can be found in most Asian grocery stores)
1   tablespoon sugar
1½   cups fresh cilantro, chopped

1.   Scrub mussels well and remove beards.
2.   Juice limes to make ⅓ cup.
3.   In a heavy saucepan, boil lime juice, coconut milk, wine, curry paste, garlic, fish sauce, and sugar over high heat, stirring, for 2 minutes.
4.   Add mussels, tossing to combine with sauce.
5.   Cook mussels, covered, stirring occasionally, until opened, about 5 to 8 minutes. (Discard any unopened mussels.)
6.   Add cilantro and toss with mussels.
7.   Serve mussels with lime wedges and crusty bread or over white rice.

Yield: 4 servings

Vegetable Panini

Prep Time: 20 minutes
Cook Time: 5-10 minutes

Panini:

1	tablespoon olive oil
1	red onion, thinly sliced
1	cup zucchini, thinly sliced
1	cup mushrooms, thinly sliced
1	cup red bell pepper, thinly sliced
1	tablespoon balsamic vinegar
1	teaspoon Dijon mustard
¼	teaspoon salt
¼	teaspoon pepper
1	loaf Focaccia bread
1	avocado, mashed
4	ounces sharp cheddar cheese
8	ounces sliced roast beef or turkey (optional)

1. Heat oil in sauté pan over medium heat.
2. Add onion, zucchini, mushrooms, red bell pepper, balsamic vinegar, and Dijon mustard.
3. Cook until the vegetables are cooked through, about 10 minutes. Add salt and pepper and set aside.
4. Cut focaccia bread horizontally and then into quarters. Spread mashed avocado over the bottom of the bread.
5. Evenly distribute the vegetable mixture between the four pieces of bread. Top with optional cheese and meat and top half of the bread.
6. Place sandwich in panini maker (if available) and cook until browned.
   If you do not have a panini maker, place sandwiches on cookie sheet and broil until the top is browned or grill in frying pan.
7. This is a very versatile recipe-you can substitute any type of meat or cheese or use no meat.

Yield: 4 servings

Portland's Forest Park

Established in 1947, Northwest Portland's Forest Park is the largest forested city park in the United States.

The park is a rustic and peaceful 5,000-acre environment overlooking the Willamette River. Many consider the Park a great quick escape from downtown because it provides quiet time for hikers, runners, bicyclists, horseback riders and other outdoor enthusiasts.

Forest Park is also home to over 100 species of mammals and more than 100 kinds of birds. In the spring, hillsides are blanketed with trilliums and later in the year hundreds of other native flowers and shrubs burst into bloom. The 30-mile long Wildwood Trail winds through the park and adds to the total of more than 70 miles of interconnecting trails and lanes that create opportunities for different levels of circle hikes.

Duniway Chocolate Sheet Cake

Prep Time: Cake-10 minutes
Frosting: 15 minutes
Cook Time: 20-30 minutes
Oven: 350 degrees

Cake:

2	cups flour	2	sticks butter
2	cups sugar	1	cup water
½	teaspoon salt	2	eggs
1	teaspoon baking soda	¼	cup buttermilk
4	1-ounce unsweetened chocolate squares	1	teaspoon vanilla

1. Preheat oven to 350 degrees.
2. In a mixing bowl, combine flour, sugar, salt and baking soda.
3. In a saucepan, melt, on low heat, chocolate, butter, and water, stirring constantly.
4. Mix melted chocolate into dry mix.
5. Add eggs and buttermilk and mix.
6. Add vanilla and mix.
7. Spray 9 x 13 cake pan with non-stick cooking spray. Pour batter into pan.
8. Bake for 20 minutes or until a toothpick inserted into middle of cake comes out clean.
9. Cool for 10 minutes.

Frosting:

12 ounces bittersweet chocolate
¾   cup butter plus ½ tablespoon
½   cup hot water
1   teaspoon corn syrup
1   tablespoon vanilla
1   cup roasted pecan pieces

1. In a saucepan or double boiler, melt chocolate over low heat. Remove from heat right before all of chocolate melts to prevent burning. Stir in ¾ cup butter, a little at a time until melted.
2. Add hot water. Stir until smooth, stir in corn syrup and vanilla. Cool.
3. Melt ½ tablespoon butter in saucepan. Roast chopped pecans over low heat. Stir constantly for 5-10 minutes to prevent burning.
4. Spread frosting onto cake. Cover with pecans.

Yield: 8-12 servings

Sweet Home Cookies

Prep Time: 15 minutes
Cook Time: 12-13 minutes
Oven: 350 degrees

Cookies:

1   cup butter, room temperature
1   cup dark brown sugar, firmly packed
½   cup granulated sugar
2   eggs
2   teaspoons vanilla
2   cups all purpose flour
1   teaspoon baking soda
½   teaspoon salt
1½ cups quick or old-fashioned oats, uncooked
½   cup coconut
1   cup corn flakes, crushed
12   ounces chocolate chips

1. Preheat oven to 350 degrees.
2. Cream together butter, brown sugar, granulated sugar, eggs and vanilla.
3. In a separate bowl sift together flour, soda and salt.
4. Add butter and sugar mixture to flour mixture.
5. Add oatmeal, coconut, corn flakes and chocolate chips and mix well.
2. Spoon onto cookie sheet.
3. Bake for 8 minutes.

Yield: 5 dozen

Oatmeal Spice Cake with Caramel Pecan Glaze

Prep Time Cake: 15 minutes
Prep Time Glaze: 15 minutes
Cook Time: 25-30 minutes
Oven: 350 degrees

Cake:

1¼	cups boiling water	1	teaspoon vanilla
1	cup oatmeal	1	cup of flour
1½	cups packed brown sugar	1	teaspoon baking soda
¾	cup butter	1	teaspoon cinnamon
2	eggs	1	teaspoon nutmeg

1. Preheat oven to 350 degrees.
2. Pour hot water over oatmeal and cover.
3. Cream brown sugar and butter.
4. Add eggs, vanilla and oatmeal. Mix well.
5. In a separate bowl, sift together flour, soda, cinnamon, and nutmeg.
6. Add to the oatmeal mixture.
7. Pour into a greased 8 x 11 pan.
8. Bake at 350 degrees for 25-30 minutes.

Glaze:

½	cup butter plus 1 tablespoon	1	cup flaked coconut
½	cup evaporated milk	½	cup pecans, chopped
1	cup brown sugar		

1. In a saucepan over low heat, melt ½ cup butter and add evaporated milk.
2. Remove from heat and stir in brown sugar and coconut.
3. In a separate saucepan, melt 1 tablespoon butter over low heat.
4. Add pecans and roast. Stirring frequently for 5-10 minutes.
5. Add pecans to glaze.
6. Spread on cake.
7. Lightly toast under broiler.

Yield: 12-16 servings

STUMPTOWN MOCHA CHEESECAKE

Prep Time: 20 minutes
Cook Time: 1 hour
Oven: 350 degrees
Chill: Overnight

CRUST:
2   cups graham cracker crumbs
2   tablespoons sugar
⅛   cup melted butter

1. Mix in a 9-inch spring form pan and pat on bottom and part way up sides.
2. Preheat oven to 350 degrees.

CHEESECAKE:
24   ounces of cream cheese at room temperature (can use low or non-fat versions)
1   cup sugar
3   eggs
½   cup sour cream
3   tablespoons flour
2   teaspoons vanilla
6   ounces chocolate chips, melted
2   tablespoons instant espresso dissolved in 1 teaspoon of hot water

1. Beat cream cheese and sugar in a large bowl until smooth and creamy, blend in eggs, sour cream, flour and vanilla.
2. Mix espresso with melted chocolate chips and swirl into the cheese mixture.
3. Pour into crust and bake at 350 degrees for 50 minutes.
4. Turn oven off, do not open the door, leave cake in the oven for 1 hour.
5. Cool completely, chill overnight.

Yield: 6-8 servings

Recipe Contributors and Testers

Writing **From Raindrops to Roses, A Collection of Oregon Style Celebrations**, brought numerous women together to develop this book as a fundraising project for the Junior League of Portland. This publication is the result of hard work and dedication from the Junior League of Portland and friends. From tasting parties to cookbook workshops, friendships were formed over food and dining.

We would like to thank these people for submitting their recipes, testing recipes, editing, and typing recipes. This book and the community projects it will fund would not be in existence without you.

Allison Abbott
Jill Anderson
Jill Arena
Kathi Austin
Lauren Ball
Lynne Bangsund
Heidi Beck
Rhonda Beck
Anne Bell
Elizabeth Bennett
Ann Blume
Channing Bosler
Kathy Brandeberry
Patty Brandt
Julie Branford
Paul Brett
Carol Brimhall
Kristen Buonpane
Beth Butrick
Jennifer Butts
Claire Calvin
Megan Campbell
Joanne Carlson
Amy Checkman
Pat Chittick
Ophelia Chiu
Dina Cole
Mara Comaianni
Andrea Costello
Laura Danna
Samantha DeJohn
Sheri Deterling
Michelle Diamond
Lori Dierckes

Cheryl Duarte
Michelle Doherty
Tracy Dudek
Andrea Dufresne
Tammy Eck
Holly Eddins
Elsie Edge
Michelle Elliott
Sandra Fairall
Kathryn Findlay
Jenny Fletcher
JoAnna Flynn
Teresa Forni
Melinda Fowler
Marsha W. Freed
Shanette Gains
Lori Geddings
Cari Goodwin
Lisa Gonsalves
Jennifer Gordon
Lynda Gordon
Deborah Grams
Kirsten Gromko
Julia Hall
Rhona Hamilton
Francis Hamrick
Lynette Heath
Lisa Hedberg
Julia Hedges
Kristin Hedman
Erica Hetfeld
Wendy Herrero
Erin Hire
Kelley Holt

Kirsten Holloway
Carrie Hoon
Lynnette Houghton
Susan Houser
Allison Howard
Deb Howes
Sara Hunt
Emily Hunt-Nelson
Nancy Hur-Crabbe
Nancy Janney
Hallie Janssen
Erica Johnson
Marina Johnson
Barbra Jorgensen
Jean Josephson
Lisa Kakishita
Terri Keener
Allison Kehoe
Kris Kern
Melinda King
Jenny Kingsbury
Jessica Klein
Patti Knollman
Molly Komenda
Amy Kranenburg
Kelly Krause
Deidre Krys-Rusoff
Annie Landfield
Kristi Langdon
Heather Leek
Sally LeFeber
Pamela Lindberg
Marilyn Lindgren
Jennifer Lynch

Mandy Magaddino
Lindsey Miles
Kyle McEligot
Mary McFarland
Amy McKinley
Lisa McNabb
Kristen Miles
Erin Mills
Myong-Hui Murphy
Kierstan Myers
Karley Nees
Katy Neill
Lola Nelson
Martha Norrie
Micki Nutt
Heather Oliver
Caroline Ozment
Jennifer Pape
Lisa Perrin
Christin Peterson
Deanna Phillips
Gretchen Pilip
Tina Pisenti
Dana Plautz
Tori Pontrelli
Mandy Ragan
Angie Regali
Annemarie Reger
Raquel Rich
Debbie Richman
Kristin Riddle
Elspeth Rogers
Judy Rompa
Robyn Ronzio

Kim Ruffer
Anne Ryan
Tege Sauer
Gina Saunders
Donna Smalldon
Kate Smith
Gail Snodgrass
Sloane Starke
Anne Stein Gray
Amy Stephens
Amber Stinson
Chris Swanson
Allison Terpening
Madeleine Toombs
Kari Tunstill
Barbara Ueltschi
Sharon Urry
Julie Vigeland
Shelley Voboril
Sandra Wagner
Christina Walker
Stacia Walker
Beth Warner
Patti Weber
Rebecca Welch
Karen Wheeler
Kaycee Wiita
Connie Wilson
Sally Wolcott
Martha Wright
Kristen Yoerger
Chrisitne Zieverink

INDEX

From Raindrops to Roses

A Collection of Oregon Style Celebrations

Junior League of Portland, Oregon Inc.
842 SW 1st Avenue
Portland, Oregon 97204
www.juniorleagueofportland.org
503-203-2372 (Phone)
503-297-8234 (Fax)
info@juniorleagueofportland.org

YOUR ORDER	QTY.	TOTAL
From Raindrops to Roses - A Collection of Oregon Style Celebrations at $24.95 per book		$
Postage and handling at $5.00 (1st book) plus $1.00 (each additional book)		$
	TOTAL	$

Name _____

Address _____

City _____ State _____ Zip _____

Telephone _____ Email _____

Method of Payment   ( ) MasterCard   ( ) Visa
( ) Check payable to Junior League of Portland

Account Number_____ Expiration Date_____ Security Number_____

Signature _____

Photocopies will be accepted

**JUNIOR LEAGUE OF
PORTLAND, OR**
Women building better communities